T0248158

THE LITTLE BOOK
OF
BITCOIN

Little Book Big Profits Series

In the Little Book series, the brightest icons in the financial world write on topics that range from tried-and-true investment strategies to tomorrow's new trends. Each book offers a unique perspective on investing, allowing the reader to pick and choose from the very best in investment advice today.

Books in the Little Book series include:

The Little Book of Investing Like the Pros by Pearl and Rosenbaum
The Little Book That Still Beats the Market by Joel Greenblatt
The Little Book That Saves Your Assets by David M. Darst
The Little Book That Builds Wealth by Pat Dorsey
The Little Book That Makes You Rich by Louis Navellier
The Little Book of Common Sense Investing by John C. Bogle
The Little Book of Value Investing by Christopher Browne
The Little Book of Big Dividends by Charles B. Carlson
The Little Book of Main Street Money by Jonathan Clements
The Little Book of Trading by Michael W. Covel
The Little Book of Valuation by Aswath Damodaran
The Little Book of Economics by Greg Ip
The Little Book of Sideways Markets by Vitaliy N. Katsenelson
The Little Book of Big Profits from Small Stocks by Hilary Kramer
The Little Book of Currency Trading by Kathy Lien
The Little Book of Bull's Eye Investing by John Mauldin
The Little Book of Emerging Markets by Mark Mobius
The Little Book of Behavioral Investing by James Montier
The Little Book of Hedge Funds by Anthony Scaramucci
The Little Book of Bull Moves by Peter D. Schiff
The Little Book of Alternative Investments by Stein and DeMuth
The Little Book of Bulletproof Investing by Ben Stein and Phil DeMuth
The Little Book of Commodity Investing by John R. Stephenson
The Little Book of the Shrinking Dollar by Addison Wiggin
The Little Book of Stock Market Profits by Mitch Zacks
The Little Book of Safe Money by Jason Zweig
The Little Book of Zen Money by The Seven Dollar Millionaire
The Little Book of Picking Top Stocks by Martin S. Fridson
The Little Book of Robo Investing by Elizabeth MacBride and Quian Liu
The Little Book of Trading Options Like the Pros by David Berns and Michael Green
The Little Book of Impact Investing by Priya Parrish
The Litte Book of Market Myths by Ken Fisher, Lara W. Hoffmans and Chris Ciarmiello
The Litte Book of Hedge Funds, Second Edition by Anthony Scaramucci

THE LITTLE BOOK

OF
BITCOIN

*What You Need to Know
that Wall Street Has Already
Figured Out*

ANTHONY SCARAMUCCI

WILEY

Published by John Wiley & Sons, Inc., Hoboken, New Jersey.
Published simultaneously in Canada.

No part of this publication may be reproduced, stored in a retrieval system, or transmitted in any form or by any means, electronic, mechanical, photocopying, recording, scanning, or otherwise, except as permitted under Section 107 or 108 of the 1976 United States Copyright Act, without either the prior written permission of the Publisher, or authorization through payment of the appropriate per-copy fee to the Copyright Clearance Center, Inc., 222 Rosewood Drive, Danvers, MA 01923, (978) 750-8400, fax (978) 750-4470, or on the web at www.copyright.com. Requests to the Publisher for permission should be addressed to the Permissions Department, John Wiley & Sons, Inc., 111 River Street, Hoboken, NJ 07030, (201) 748-6011, fax (201) 748-6008, or online at http://www.wiley.com/go/permission.

Trademarks: Wiley and the Wiley logo are trademarks or registered trademarks of John Wiley & Sons, Inc. and/or its affiliates in the United States and other countries and may not be used without written permission. All other trademarks are the property of their respective owners. John Wiley & Sons, Inc. is not associated with any product or vendor mentioned in this book.

Limit of Liability/Disclaimer of Warranty: While the publisher and author have used their best efforts in preparing this book, they make no representations or warranties with respect to the accuracy or completeness of the contents of this book and specifically disclaim any implied warranties of merchantability or fitness for a particular purpose. No warranty may be created or extended by sales representatives or written sales materials. The advice and strategies contained herein may not be suitable for your situation. You should consult with a professional where appropriate. Further, readers should be aware that websites listed in this work may have changed or disappeared between when this work was written and when it is read. Neither the publisher nor authors shall be liable for any loss of profit or any other commercial damages, including but not limited to special, incidental, consequential, or other damages.

For general information on our other products and services or for technical support, please contact our Customer Care Department within the United States at (800) 762-2974, outside the United States at (317) 572-3993 or fax (317) 572-4002.

Wiley also publishes its books in a variety of electronic formats. Some content that appears in print may not be available in electronic formats. For more information about Wiley products, visit our web site at www.wiley.com.

Library of Congress Cataloging-in-Publication Data is Available:

ISBN 9781394286645 (Cloth)
ISBN 9781394286652 (ePDF)
ISBN 9781394286669 (ePub)

COVER DESIGN: PAUL MCCARTHY

SKY10087147_100824

Contents

Foreword

———————— ∾ ————————

In the 20th century, the global financial system was built on familiar assets—real estate, stocks, and bonds—all functioning within legacy systems designed for a world that moved at the pace of telephone wires and trading floors. Wealth was managed through a network of trusted intermediaries: governments, banks, and corporations that assured the safe custody and growth of capital. Yet, the twenty-first century brings with it new expectations—a world where speed, intelligence, and resilience are paramount, and where the younger generation seeks a financial system as dynamic as the technology that defines their lives.

Capital is the lifeblood of this economic engine—a force that drives innovation, growth, and prosperity. In its quest for optimal allocation, capital must flow seamlessly among investors, corporations, money managers, and entrepreneurs. While many assets can store capital, only a select few possess the qualities—liquidity, durability, divisibility, portability, and fungibility—that elevate them to the status of money.

In the nineteenth century, gold was the cornerstone of this system. It was the ultimate store of value, revered for its scarcity and stability. However, as the twentieth century unfolded, it became clear that gold, despite its merits, could not keep pace with an increasingly interconnected and fast-moving global economy. The world needed a more agile and responsive form of money, leading to the adoption of the U.S. dollar as the global reserve currency, backed by U.S. Treasury Bills rather than gold.

Gold, while stable, is inherently inflationary—its supply increases by approximately 2% per year. This gradual dilution of value forces holders to seek productive investments that yield returns sufficient to outpace inflation. For decades, the dollar, linked to gold and later free-floating, promised a similar stability with greater utility in a growing global economy. But with the end of the Bretton Woods system in 1971, the world entered an era of fiat currency, where the dollar's value was no longer tethered to a physical asset.

Central banks and economists aimed to manage this new system by controlling inflation, targeting an annual rate of 2%—a synthetic attempt to mimic the slow and steady inflation of gold. However, this approach proved far more complex in practice. Inflation is difficult to measure accurately and even harder to control. The metrics used—CPI, PPI, PCE—are imperfect and frequently revised, making comparisons across time unreliable. In reality, since the abandonment of the gold standard, the U.S. dollar has experienced inflation rates ranging from 7–10% annually, with weaker currencies suffering even more.

For families, corporations, and governments capitalized in these currencies, the long-term erosion of value is staggering. A currency with 7% inflation loses nearly all its purchasing power over a century. In economies with higher inflation, this loss occurs within a single generation. Investors understand that holding cash or government debt is a losing strategy, yet many corporations and institutions are constrained by regulations and traditions that limit their options, resulting in a consistent erosion of real returns.

For those in the developing world, the challenges are even greater. Entrepreneurs and institutions must navigate unstable currencies, unreliable banking systems, and political risks that can wipe out savings overnight. The traditional financial system, with its cumbersome processes and limited accessibility, is ill-suited to meet the needs of a world that operates at the speed of the internet.

This is where Bitcoin enters the scene—a technology born from the recognition that the twenty-first century demands a new form of money, one that is not just faster and smarter but fundamentally stronger. When Satoshi Nakamoto introduced Bitcoin, he did more than create a digital currency; he reimagined the very concept of money. By enabling the transfer and custody of assets without the need for trusted intermediaries, Bitcoin established itself as the first true digital commodity—an asset that exists purely in cyberspace, untethered from the physical and political constraints of the traditional financial system.

Bitcoin's breakthrough lies in its deflationary nature—a fixed supply of 21 million coins ensures that it is immune to the inflationary pressures that plague fiat currencies and even gold. This design elevates Bitcoin from a mere digital asset to a revolutionary form of money, one that conserves economic energy across both space and time. Unlike any other asset in history, Bitcoin offers the possibility of perpetual value preservation.

Imagine moving vast sums of money across the globe in seconds, or storing wealth that can last not just for decades but for centuries. Bitcoin's decentralized network operates continuously, enabling seamless, instant transactions between any two entities, anywhere in the world. It is not just a new form of money; it is a new financial infrastructure—one that is open to all, resilient against censorship, and capable of powering an economy that operates at the speed of light.

But perhaps the most profound impact of Bitcoin is its ability to preserve value over time. Traditional assets degrade;

their economic life is limited by inflation, depreciation, and mismanagement. In contrast, Bitcoin's maintenance costs are minuscule, making it the first asset with the potential for economic immortality. As a primary treasury reserve asset, Bitcoin can extend the life span of corporations, institutions, and even governments, ensuring that wealth is preserved and protected for future generations.

With Bitcoin, humanity has taken a monumental step forward—from slow, sound metallic money to fast, weak financial money, to the dawn of a stronger, faster, and smarter digital money. We are entering the era of sound money once again, but this time, it is built for the digital age.

The future is not just bright—it is transformative.

—Michael Saylor, CEO MicroStrategy

About the Foreword Author

———————— ∽ ————————

Wʜᴇɴ Mɪᴄʜᴀᴇʟ Sᴀʏʟᴏʀ ᴡᴀsɴ'ᴛ seeing into the future, he was dreaming of it.

The son of a career Air Force officer, Saylor moved around a lot as he grew up on various military bases. He was always fascinated by aeronautics and the promise of what the future held. Like many children of that era, Saylor wanted to be an astronaut or fighter pilot, or perhaps even a rock star. When not directly pursuing those goals, he'd spend hours exploring the worlds created by science-fiction greats Arthur C. Clark and Isaac Asimov. The stories may have been fantastical, but there was a real message in all of them: technology can make tomorrow possible.

A standout student, Saylor scored 1540 out of a possible 1600 on his SAT and enrolled at MIT, where he double majored in aeronautics and science. To pay for college, Saylor joined the Air Force Reserve Officer Training Corps. It was a dream come true. After all, this was during the time of *Top Gun* when nothing was more glamorous than flying an F-16. One could argue that is still the case. A mistaken medical diagnosis prevented him from fulfilling that dream, and when budget cuts sent him into the reserves, Saylor found himself jobless. But the setback sent him on a new trajectory, one that would take him to even greater heights: entrepreneur.

Through a friend, Saylor found a job in software working for DuPont. He immediately impressed, and before long, at the age of 24, the company gave him office space and funds to start his new business: MicroStrategy. It would be the last place he would ever work. It would also go on to make him a billionaire many times over. Saylor recognized early just how powerful software could be in helping companies become leaner and more efficient at using information and data to make business decisions.

I first met Saylor over Zoom during the pandemic, well after he had established himself as a voice of authority in the Bitcoin community. The fabulous Peter Briger, a Fortress partner and a Bitcoin OG, introduced us. In advance of our meeting, I read his 2012 book, *The Mobile Wave*, and immediately proceeded to flog myself for not reading it earlier. I would've made a fortune. In it, Saylor laid out why Facebook, Amazon,

Apple, and Google were going to decimate the world. You see, Saylor understood what differentiated a Palm Pilot from an Apple iPhone, why Facebook was different from Myspace. In his view, those companies allowed software to jump from a computer to a handset, or as he described it, from a solid state to a vapor one. Software would no longer exist on a computer; it would follow us, sleep with and always surround us. In his view, these tech giants weren't even companies – they were networks. Networks for retail (Amazon), networks for social outlets (Facebook, now Meta), networks for information (Google, now Alphabet). They were vehicles that dematerialized products and services. Instead of a physical map, you could have a virtual one that could not only offer you directions but also give you the latest traffic info. Goodbye Thomas Guide, goodbye shadow traffic reporter on the radio. Now, with an iPhone, you could snap photos of yourself and instantly send it to a friend, with comments! Goodbye cameras. Goodbye film. Goodbye postcards.

These companies were going to destroy or change every industry they touched. And they were going to make a fortune doing so. With Apple, Facebook, and Google trading at all-year highs in the early 2010s and every investor screaming "bubble," Saylor ignored the prices of these behemoths and instead focused on the factors that were driving them. He proceeded to buy $50 million worth of those stocks. He turned it into $500 million.

The move netted him a small fortune, but it did something else, it awakened a simple investment principle that would guide him, and it was this: if you want to make money, find a dominant digital network and invest in it, and then invest in it some more. Eventually, all the doubters, all the haters, all the people who mocked it and didn't understand the technology, who applied traditional metrics to a never-before-seen asset, those same people would have to come around, because not owning those networks would be tantamount to shorting the market.

But Saylor's success was not without regrets, albeit high-quality ones. He regretted not buying more, and he regretted ever selling. Most investors would be thrilled with making 10 times their money. And to be fair, Saylor was. But what bothered him most was that in his gut he knew these companies were more than just stocks. They were change agents. They represented physical shares in progress, in the future he always held dear. So, to Saylor, selling, or not buying more, didn't represent a prudent financial decision. In some ways it was the opposite. He let price, not promise, determine his actions.

He had another regret as well.

While the investment was a personal success, his company didn't participate, and that missed opportunity left a lasting impression on him. He made a promise to himself.

If ever there were a transformative technology to come around again, he wouldn't simply buy a position and write a book about it. No, he would never make that mistake again. Instead, he would buy it personally and corporately and then tweet about it religiously.

Bitcoin would be that second chance.

He initially wasn't a big supporter of Bitcoin; in fact, he was very skeptical of it in the early days. But once he did come around, he realized the future of value was staring him right in the face, something that even his science-fiction heroes could never have imagined, and he would go all in, more so than he had with Apple and Amazon a decade ago. Bitcoin displayed many of the same traits as those companies. It was disruptive. It dematerialized entrenched industries. It was universally doubted and mocked by many. And it was going higher. But this time, he wouldn't just buy it personally; he would extend MicroStrategy's treasury and add Bitcoin to the company's balance sheet and, in doing so, make the boldest statement yet about where he thought this new asset class was going.

And again, he was right.

I've had the privilege to get to know Michael both professionally and personally. I'm proud to call him a colleague, but I'm prouder to call him a friend. Michael has a gifted mind. It doesn't work like ours. My brain is a Mercedes.

His is a Bugatti. He sees things that others don't and can explain them in simple terms that others can't. He's been a terrific ambassador to the Coin. He's been a trusted source of wisdom for me. He's a genius, and I don't use that term lightly. I cannot thank him enough for guiding me through this new and exciting world. And I could not be happier to include him in this book.

Preface

—————————— ∾ ——————————

Great investments don't come around too often. But when they do, it's like magic. They can create generational wealth. They can also make up for the many bad investments you've made or likely will make over your lifetime. I know they have for me. Think Nike in the 1980s. Microsoft in the 1990s. Apple in the 2000s. Tesla in the 2010s. You get the picture here. Transformational companies that create new industries while disrupting old ones. The story was staring you right in the face. You could see the price action, but for whatever reason, you didn't invest, or more accurately, you didn't invest enough. The train left the station without you and the untold millions you would've made.

If only.

I know this feeling. I know it well, and if we're being honest, you probably know it, too. I was lucky that I didn't make the same mistake with Bitcoin, although after reading this book you'll learn just how close I came to missing out on that one as well. I first learned about Bitcoin in 2012. It was just the beginning of the mobile Internet. Technology was just beginning to shape the lives we now know. Facebook. Amazon. Google. These companies were just starting to assert their dominance in ways investors had never imagined even 5 or 10 years earlier. Some called them overvalued. Many credited their surging stock prices to ultra-low interest rates. They were considered tech stocks, but as the world would later find out, those companies would impact every aspect of our lives. Now everything is tech, or tech adjacent. Name one major company whose business you don't interact with using a smartphone. In short, these handful of companies changed the world, and investors in them were handsomely rewarded. But by the time everyone realized the full impact, the majority of the gains had been made.

I'd like to think when I first learned about Bitcoin that I was smart enough to realize its potential. I did not, at least initially. I took the same jaundiced eye that many traditional Wall Streeters took. Digital Internet money? Yeah, right! You have to remember, I'm the son of Italian immigrants who grew up on Long Island in the 1960s and 1970s. I'm hard-wired to detect a scam or anything that could separate me or my customers from our hard-earned cash. I'm also a 30-year veteran of Wall Street who worked at places like Goldman Sachs and Neuberger Berman. Even when I struck out to start my own asset management firm, I was still very much part of the traditional financial system. I knew stocks, bonds, derivatives, FX, and all the traditional investments, and I knew them well. What I did not know in 2012 was that I was staring at possibly the greatest investment of all time. A once-in-a-lifetime opportunity. Better even than Apple or Amazon circa 2000. The investment equivalent of fire or the wheel. Unfortunately, it took me eight years until I realized that, but when I did, I fully jumped into the world of the Coin.

Of course, few journeys are taken alone. And I was blessed to be guided by some of the best investors in the world. Some were friends. Some became friends. But they are all legends. In this book, you'll hear their stories, too. People like Michael Saylor. Peter Briger. Michael Novogratz. Wences Casares. The Bitcoin OGs. These people are all investors and entrepreneurs who saw the power of this new technology and moved before anyone else. You'll learn how they were able to see the future and have the courage to go not just against conventional wisdom but also against some of the biggest names in finance, the Bitcoin haters. The Jamie Dimons of the world. Warren Buffett. Charlie Munger. In a business where reputation is everything, the Bitcoin

OGs were willing to risk it all. Their conviction inspired me to do the same. So, in 2020, when I transitioned SkyBridge from a traditional Wall Street, fund-of-funds business into a Bitcoin firm, I knew I was risking more than just my money. I was risking my reputation. But after learning about this new asset class, I knew the risks of not jumping in were far greater than playing it safe. Trust me when I say it wasn't easy. I took more than my fair share of hits, snide comments, and invective from the establishment financial community. I ignored them. True wealth is created not by seeking the approval of others. True wealth is found when you make your own path.

And that's one of the reasons I wrote this book. Beyond a simple understanding of how Bitcoin works, or why it should be a part of anyone's portfolio, what I hope this book also teaches you is how to see beyond the clutter and distractions that too often impede our financial decisions. Letting outside opinions determine your own can lead to dire consequences, both personally and professionally. There may be safety in crowds, but a herd mentality can be dangerous to your money. The brilliant investors who thumbed their nose at Bitcoin weren't stupid or incapable of understanding how it worked. I suspect in most cases their aversion to Bitcoin had more to do with how they perceived their involvement may tarnish their reputations. Could a billionaire many times over admit to possibly being wrong about maybe the world's greatest invention, reverse course, and jump in after a bunch of retail investors already had? Perhaps when you get that rich, the only thing that really matters is your reputation. Fortunately, most of us don't have that problem and, as a result, we have the opportunity to profit from what I believe is the next great asset class.

Next great asset class? Yes, without a doubt. I've never been more convicted professionally about anything. Now, you might be thinking, "Mooch, slow down! There's no such thing as a sure bet." And for the most part you are correct. I'm probably one of the most conservative investors you'll ever meet. But as you will learn from this book, Bitcoin solves many of the traditional problems fiat money has encountered through the centuries. It's a perfect medium of value, and after reading this book, you'll understand why. You'll know how to invest in Bitcoin, and the role it needs to play in your portfolio, no matter what type of investor you happen to be. Most important, you'll understand why, despite massive gains, Bitcoin's ascension is still very much in its infancy. I know that may sound crazy given its incredible run. Since it was first mined on January 3, 2009, it's gone from basically a penny to more than $70000 a coin. At any point along the way, it was way too easy to liken it to previous bubbles, whether it be tulips or tech stocks in the 1990s. The harder, contrarian approach would've been to try to understand why Bitcoin was going up. Of course, Bitcoin has had plenty of crashes, too, but after reading this book, you'll understand why that's a good thing. It has overcome its fair share of bad actors, governments, and regulatory agencies that have tried to cripple or ban it outright. And yet each time it comes back, only stronger and more essential to the global financial system.

People fear that which they don't understand, and that fear prevents us from making rational decisions, whether we're talking about investments or even personal matters. If you don't understand something, it's easier to ignore and dismiss it. But doing so suppresses your instinct to understand new and exciting possibilities, whether they be technology or potential investment opportunities. Fear of the unknown can cause you to settle into old routines. But that's not where fortunes lay. Investors often need to unlearn that which they have spent years learning. People fear Bitcoin because it is a new technology, because it was created outside the financial system, and because it has the power to disrupt traditional finance in ways the industry has never seen. That's why some of the brightest minds and biggest institutions have jumped in. Larry Fink's BlackRock is quickly dominating the market for Bitcoin spot exchange-traded funds (ETFs) not because he fears the future but rather because he embraces it.

And after reading this book, not only will you understand how Bitcoin works, but I suspect you'll want to jump in, too.

THE LITTLE BOOK

OF
BITCOIN

Chapter One

Introduction

"Dad, you're technologically tone deaf. You can barely turn on your iPhone." It was my son, AJ, and he was just about to give me some of the best advice of my life.

"When I say 'blockchain,' you have no idea what I'm talking about," he complained. "When I say, 'The Internet of Things,' you're clueless!"

My son, who was working at Tesla during the summer of 2012, urged me to get with the times.

"You have to address this," he added. By "this," he meant that I was a technology luddite.

He suggested I fix "this" by enrolling in an executive class at Singularity University. Despite the name, Singularity isn't really a university at all. It's not an accredited institution. It doesn't dole out diplomas. Instead, it offers something way more useful: a glimpse into the future.

Founded by futurists and entrepreneurs Ray Kurzweil and Peter Diamandis, Singularity University's promise is simple: "Don't fear the future – own it."

And so, in April 2013, I enrolled at the sprawling NASA Ames Research Center in the heart of California's Silicon Valley. Singularity offers professionals weekly courses that combine the best elements of think tanks, seminars, and conferences. You learn from and network with some of the brightest and most forward-thinking minds in tech.

It was then when I first learned about the world of block-chain digital assets, particularly Bitcoin.

Diamandis was speaking along with Hal Finney, who, in addition to being one of the early developers of console gaming, was one of the first Bitcoin adopters. In fact, he was the recipient of the very first Bitcoin transaction. Finney was an early believer in digital currencies, having experimented with its earliest forms like DigiCash. But those protocols were centralized, and in Bitcoin he had finally found a real free and decentralized currency. Now he was teaching others.

The two talked less about the coin itself and more about the factors that were driving it or what Diamandis called

"The Six Ds of Exponentials," which he viewed as the keys to identifying lucrative long-term investment ideas. These are Digitize, Dematerialize, Demonetize, Democratize, Deception, and finally Disruption.

In Diamandis' view, if you can digitize a product or service, you can effectively dematerialize it, reducing the physical to metadata, or a series of ones and zeros. And moving from a physical to a virtual good or service is a much more efficient process since now everything is just data. Digitizing a product makes it cheaper and more universally available; it's now democratized, and everyone can have it. Before you know it, it's deceptively become a disruptive force in its industry.

What he was really talking about is how to identify technologies that have the power to disrupt, redefine, and then scale up various industries. Diamandis called this phenomenon "exponential technologies," and it didn't apply to the small stuff, like a color versus a black-and-white television. He was more interested in discovering and harnessing the airwaves that made television possible. Think electricity. Mobility. Computers. The next great technology that immediately changes every industry it touches. The Internet! And now he was looking at a new one that had been around only a couple years and was viewed by many with a cynical eye.

"Kodak made the epic error of thinking they were in the chemicals and paper business," Diamandis told his class.

"They thought that because that's where they made their profits, and anything not in service to that was a waste." The problem was that digital photography was on an exponential growth curve.

"So, when the digital camera came along, Kodak executives took a look at the standard 0.01 megapixel camera and laughed at it. But the next year it was 0.02 megapixels. Then 0.04. Then 0.08. And after 30 doublings, it was better than the standard traditional camera, and Kodak was bankrupt," Diamandis explained.

His point was simple: moving from the physical to the virtual is a wildly disruptive and potentially lucrative process, both for goods and for services. But it's a necessary one if a company or industry is going to evolve and survive. Those that don't transition are inevitably eaten by technology as industries become leaner and more efficient. Think about all the physical goods you probably kept in your home just 25 years ago. You likely had a landline phone, which required lots of plastic and cords. You may have even had an answering machine. You probably had a stereo system, with a stack of CDs next to it. You had a camera, maybe a digital one but likely an old-fashioned film one that required you to take that roll and have it developed. And let's not forget the TV, which required a cable box but also probably had a nice stack of DVDs sitting not too far from those CDs. Most, if not all, of those devices have been reduced to a series of ones and zeros. They've become digitized, combined, and reimaged into one remarkable device: the smartphone. Your phone now carries your pictures, music, movies, and phone (to say nothing of your computer). All that physical stuff now fits into the palm of your hand. And as a result, Apple's $3 trillion market capitalization is bigger than Germany's entire stock market and half that of Japan's. Staggering change creates – and destroys – stupendous value.

In fairness to the good folks at Kodak, digital photography looked like a loser and in fact was a loser at the time. Shifting from a profitable business to an unprofitable one won't exactly endear management with shareholders. But what they didn't realize is that digitization wasn't just the future. It was their lifeline. It led to the dematerialization of cameras and film. And it demonetized the process of taking photos so that, today, most of us take pictures for free. And soon enough, it democratized photography. There are eight billion phones around the world, and Kodak, Polaroid, and Nikon are all obsolete. An entire industry was reduced to a series of ones and zeros. In 2000, Kodak announced that 80 billion photos were taken, a record. In 2022, an estimated 1.5 trillion photos were taken.

"Bitcoin is digital photography," Diamandis added. "Before you know it, it will digitize and dematerialize the entire financial system, and the same thing that happened to Kodak will happen to many traditional financial institutions."

The room fell silent.

I have to be honest; I didn't really understand much of it. I knew, liked, and respected Diamandis; we were about the same age, both first-generation sons of immigrants, both from Long Island. He's wickedly smart and doesn't take himself too seriously, which are rare qualities. And it was hard to argue with the logic of what he was saying.

Still, it seemed a leap too far. I was a traditional finance guy with 25 years of experience working for places like Goldman Sachs and Neuberger Berman. The idea that money could exist outside the government seemed almost farcical to me. How could something that wasn't sanctioned by the government be considered "money" and eventually replace the dollar? How could money exist entirely in nonphysical form? For thousands of years, the construct of money was based on physical objects – coins, bills, metals. And now society was going to ignore that and accept an idea of money but without having the money? What were these guys talking about?

I left the seminar chuckling to myself, and then I promptly did what I've probably done too many times before in my life. I put my digital foot in my digital mouth and immediately took to Twitter and mocked it:

"For the record, I don't know what a #bitcoin is and could careless. Caveat Emptor," I proudly tweeted.

Buyer beware!

Do you know what embarrasses me about those 15 words as I sit here today? It's not the typo – I could "careless" about that. It's not the millions I would've made had I bought in right then. It's not even that I could have jumped up a notch or two on my son's cool-o-meter. It's that I had closed my mind.

As you go on this journey with me, into what I now believe is one of the most transformative and potentially lucrative asset classes of all time, I ask only one thing: don't repeat my mistake. Whether you're a believer or a skeptic, be open to the possibility that you could be wrong. The world may be bigger – and may be changing faster – than you previously thought. Keep an open mind, and your world can expand.

Mine was about to.

Chapter Two

Time to Go Exploring

"I'M TELLING YOU, MOOCH," said the great Mike Novogratz, pausing for effect while looking straight at me with his steely blue eyes. "It's nothing short of a cultural revolution."

When Novogratz speaks, I listen.

He's a legend – former Goldman Partner, former president of investment behemoth Fortress, but, most important, the owner of one of the clearest and most rigorous minds on Wall Street. He was also one of the few traditional finance voices who could see the future of potential. In 2018 he ventured out into the Wild West of Bitcoin and started his own crypto investment firm, Galaxy Investment Partners.

Today it's worth billions. He's also a good friend and has been for more than 20 years.

"There's nothing like it," he added.

It was 2019 and Novogratz had invited me to dinner at the Explorers Club, a society that promotes science and exploration. Past members include James Cameron, Walter Cronkite, and Neil Armstrong. It's not for the faint of heart. The headquarters are in a six-story Jacobean mansion that's jammed packed with artifacts from around the world. Skis used to cross the arctic. Taxidermy. Spacesuits. Relics from faraway places found by fearless explorers. That night, Novogratz and I were on a different sort of journey.

"It's a fascinating industry," I said, obviously understating all that was happening in crypto. "I'm just not sure how viable it is for traditional investors."

At that point, I would describe myself as deeply crypto-curious. Even after telling the world I didn't care about Bitcoin, something about it just kept pulling me back. Somehow, I knew that there was still something I didn't know. It wasn't just that crypto speculation – almost entirely from noninstitutional investors – was generating social media chatter. I could sense that something deeper was going on.

"There is an energy to this space that I have not seen in a long time. And the more I've dug in, the more excited I've become," Novogratz said. "The thing is, it's not just about Bitcoin. It's a revolution in economics. It's a revolution in the decentralized world."

Novogratz himself was first introduced to Bitcoin during his time at Fortress, when a partner on the West Coast told him about how everyone in Silicon Value was talking about this new cryptocurrency called Bitcoin. Somewhat intrigued, Novogratz started doing some research of his own and instantly saw the perfect ingredients for a speculative bubble.

"There were lots of libertarians in it," Novogratz would later recall. "Lots of antigovernment people in it. The Chinese were just looking at it, and my first instinct was to just play it for fun."

At first, Novogratz took a small position in his personal account just so he could dabble and learn about it – but like many traders, he lost interest in the space when Bitcoin began to falter. In 2015, Novogratz left Fortress, but he still had a number of crypto investments in his personal account. Not really knowing what to do with it, he called up his college roommate, Joe Lubin, who was one of the key guys building out the Ethereum project, a rival cryptocurrency, and asked if he could meet him at his Bushwick offices in Brooklyn to talk about his investments.

He went to his office expecting to see him, his dog, and maybe an assistant. Instead, he saw 30 dynamic young people crammed into a warehouse, coding, talking on the phone, and making plans for the revolution.

It was like the early days of Nasdaq over-the-counter trading – wild and brimming with unfettered confidence.

Novogratz's instinct for trading kicked in, and he immediately scooped up a bunch of Ethereum at $1 before going on an extended trip to India. When he returned, it was worth $5.

Years later, Novogratz's excitement and enthusiasm for the space were never stronger.

"This community says there is a different way of doing things. I think the punchline gets missed with everyone focusing on Bitcoin," he would later say. "The revolution is really about moving to the decentralized world."

Like many early investors, Novogratz was drawn to Bitcoin by its potential to disrupt the traditional financial services industry. And as a keen observer of macroeconomic trends, he was also aware that central banks around the world seemed to be in a continuous race to debase their own currencies. But his focus wasn't on the money. Instead, it was on the enormous amount of young intellectual capital that was flowing into this field.

"These really smart MIT and Harvard students, they don't want Goldman Sachs. They don't want Bank of America," said Novogratz. "They want this," he said, holding up his phone and pointing to the latest quote of Bitcoin.

It was while talking to Novogratz that I first realized how big this thing really was. This wasn't just a trade. It was so much deeper, so much more revolutionary. There in the Explorers Club, a few feet away from a huge stuffed polar bear, I realized something: I had to pivot my firm.

When I started SkyBridge, few, if any, companies were doing what we did. We were a fund-of-funds business, which meant we pooled smaller investors' money and invested those funds in much bigger hedge funds that they otherwise would never be able to access. In some ways, it democratized investing. A family office could now have access to Dan Loeb's Third Point or Steve Cohen's Point 72 – the best and most creative investors around.

Of course, the model was quickly copied, which, to be honest, is just Wall Street's way of telling you what a great idea you had. Doing something new means you might fall on your face. But other times, it's amazing how quickly ridicule turns to imitation. My point is, I've never been scared of being ahead of the pack.

But jumping headstrong into Bitcoin presented a problem. From a strategic point of view, one of the stupidest things you can do is transition from a traditional finance firm into a crypto one, particularly with Bitcoin at or near all-time highs. After all, there was no shortage of Bitcoin haters and, for me personally, having come off a tumultuous and short White House stint, no shortage of Scaramucci haters, too. Put the two together and you're now a walking target. But the potential was just too great. And when I realized how dramatically Bitcoin could change the financial game, I realized that the risks of doing nothing had never been greater.

Chapter Three

The World's Most Profitable Paddleboard Lesson

REMEMBER BLOCKBUSTER?

It grew from a single store in Dallas, Texas, to the leading home rental video company, with nearly 9000 stores around the world and $6 billion in sales in 2004. It was a retail behemoth, a literal blockbuster that completely dominated its market. Its business model was relatively straightforward: charge for rentals, and charge even more for late and rewind fees. In fact, in 2000, the company made $800 million in late fees, nearly 16% of its revenue. The company traded on the New York Stock Exchange under the ticker BBI and had nearly 100 000 employees. The moat around them was seemingly complete. Who could ever challenge their dominance?

So in 1997, when a tiny little mail-in DVD company called Netflix was founded by two Silicon Valley veterans who were frustrated by those very same late fees, few at Blockbuster gave it much thought. Three years later, when those same two cofounders, Marc Randolph and Reed Hastings, approached Blockbuster about buying the fast-growing start-up for $50 million, chief executive officer (CEO) at the time John Antioco "laughed them out of the room," commenting later to the press that the "dot-com hysteria" was completely "overblown."

Today, Blockbuster has one store in Bend, Oregon. Netflix is a $300-billion giant that has disrupted theaters, studios, television, and cable.

Interestingly enough, Antioco was not entirely wrong. There was an Internet bubble. Valuations in 2000 were through the roof. But what he failed to see was that Netflix, which at that time was only mailing DVDs and had yet to even think about streaming, was already disrupting its business.

He didn't realize that Blockbuster was the horse and buggy, and Netflix was the automobile. By 2010, just 10 years after Netflix approached them about being acquired, Blockbuster filed for bankruptcy.

I know many people – and particularly those who are already rich and successful – abide by the old adage "If it ain't broke, don't fix it." But the better advice is this: If it ain't broke, break it! Apple disrupted itself by replacing its wildly popular iPod with the even more wildly popular iPhone, which went on to become the most popular device in the history of the world. Netflix, which owned the mail-in DVD space, totally disrupted its own business several years later by introducing streaming, which negated the need to rent DVDs, the very heart of its business. Several years after that, it became the biggest content creator in the world and toppled Hollywood. Start to finish, in 20 years, it displaced an entire industry. It was Kodak all over again. A dominant physical business was reduced and decimated by a series of ones and zeros.

Bitcoin is Netflix. Bitcoin is the iPhone. Bitcoin is the inevitable pull of progress that will level everything in its wake. You either ride that wave or get ridden.

"I don't want to miss this," I told my colleagues. "If we are not going to do this, we need to have reasons why we aren't. And then we have to solve for those."

Before we could launch a fund, we had to be 100% comfortable in three key areas: scale, regulation, and storage.

And so, for the next two years, my partners and I researched Bitcoin and crypto as deeply as we could. We read everything we could find that was related to Bitcoin and the history of money. Through our extensive network, we set up meetings with the best and brightest investors and economists. We met with crypto industry leaders, including Novogratz and the Winklevoss twins of *The Social Network* fame, who went on to create Gemini, a leading crypto firm. We needed to get as comfortable with the world of Bitcoin as we were with the world of equities.

By late 2020, we were all working from home during COVID-19. I set up a meeting. It was me, my partner and co-chief investment officer Brett Messing, my head of research John Svolos, and other members of SkyBridge, and we were about to announce to the world that we were going to offer a Bitcoin fund.

Messing had been a driving force in pushing SkyBridge further into the world of Bitcoin and crypto. Although Messing had only been with SkyBridge for a couple years, I have known him since Harvard and from Oscar Capital Management, an asset management firm I founded in the mid-1990s. Messing is an incredibly smart, capable, and technically gifted investor.

But like much of the Street, he, too, started as more of a Bitcoin skeptic. He first heard about Bitcoin in 2014 from the chief technology officer at his previous hedge fund. He made some initial modest bets in his personal account, but the collapse of a prominent crypto exchange and the subsequent crash in Bitcoin convinced him that the industry was too speculative and nascent to be taken seriously by professional investors. After he joined SkyBridge, at my request, he took a number of meetings with important members of the crypto community, but his lingering concerns about storage and regulations still placed him firmly in the skeptic camp. The crypto culture also seemed anathema to his analytical mind. He was cautious and conservative by nature. He was not a HODLer (Bitcoin parlance for Hold On for Dear Life).

But he had been doing years of homework on the subject and remained deeply curious about the space, so when he came to me and said we needed to urgently move on Bitcoin in the late summer of 2020, I knew I had to listen.

"I had lunch with Briger, and I've never been more certain of anything," said Messing.

Peter Briger is the co-chairman of Fortress, one of the world's biggest and most successful financial firms in the world. He had rented a house up the street from Messing's in Malibu, and the two quickly became paddleboard partners during the summer of COVID. On one of their socially distanced rides, the subject of Bitcoin came up.

"What do you think of Bitcoin?" Briger asked Messing. "Because I own a lot of it."

Messing knew Briger was one of the early Bitcoin evangelists, which was something that always struck Messing as odd. After all, here was one the great vulture investors of his generation, a man who built his fortune through the arduous process of shifting through the balance sheets of troubled companies, finding some overlooked physical assets, buying up debt for 35 cents on the dollar, and hoping to sell it at 80 four or five years later. That same person, who was perfectly fluent in the arcane language of senior and subordinated tranches of distressed bonds, who made fortunes running out the clock against his opponents, was now praising an asset that critics lambasted as having no intrinsic value, no valuation metrics, and, according to many traditional investors, no "real value" at all.

"It's something that we've been looking at closely," said Messing. "But I still have a lot of questions about it."

Messing had technical concerns about the logistics of owning Bitcoin on behalf of investors. But he also had serious concerns about the mania that was beginning to surround the crypto space in mid-to-late 2020. It seemed that there was a new coin being created every second, and it was apparent that some were just flat-out scams. But to Briger, that was actually a sign of Bitcoin's strength.

"That's the resilience of Bitcoin," said Briger, growing ever more animated as he wafted over the waves. "You just had 30 000 so-called competitors enter the space, and you still see the Bitcoin adoption. With Bitcoin, it all comes down to security and sovereignty."

His thesis was relatively straightforward.

"It's really simple," said Briger, while gently riding the tide on his board. "This thing is going to continue to be adopted, the supply is limited, and eventually more institutions will want it. And the price will go higher."

He was particularly attracted to the power Bitcoin had to disrupt the margins of the banking oligopoly that is the financial services industry. In his view, the entire world was awash in innovation, from the Internet to the smartphone, except for one field. Banking.

"We have smartphones and the ability to have everybody bank at much lower costs, yet interchange and payments still cost pretty much what they did 20 or 25 years ago, because the oligopoly has not let costs come down," said Briger.

Briger was 100% correct. The financial service industry had gotten lazy or greedy or both. Most of the innovation in the banking sector hadn't actually come from banks. They came from Silicon Valley upstarts who salivated at the prospect of disrupting the margins at traditional financial institutions.

What traditional banks are really good at, maybe better than any other legacy industry, is using the regulatory infrastructure to defend their products and margins. And they can do that because the government allows them to operate as regulated oligopolies. The government insures deposits, so when rates go up, banks make even more money because they can attract even more cash.

But in Briger's view, if you can obviate that whole infrastructure and you can transact peer-to-peer with minimal friction and absolute financial security, you've created a wonderfully disruptive and potentially lucrative technology.

At this point in time, a number of generationally successful investors were announcing large stakes in Bitcoin, usually to a captive audience on CNBC's Squawk Box. Peter Thiel called it one of the most stupidly obvious trades and likened it to digital gold. In fact, he noted that the concept of owning Bitcoin was so obvious that most institutional investors would probably miss it.

And he wasn't alone. People like Stan Druckenmiller and Bill Miller, last names synonymous with success, came out in raging support of an asset class that was crashing up in the summer of 2020. Still, there seemed to be a herd mentality developing around the space, and buying Bitcoin in 2020 seemed a lot like buying Microsoft at the top in 1999.

Briger glanced out at the serene Pacific Ocean. "It's a beautiful thing."

Messing would later joke that it was the world's most lucrative paddleboard session.

At lunch that same day, Briger told Messing how he discovered Bitcoin. It was through a guy named Wences Casares, an Argentinean tech entrepreneur who helped launch Argentina's first Internet provider, Internet Argentina. Wences later founded an online brokerage firm that he sold to Banco Santander in 2000 for more than half a billion.

He was raised on a sheep ranch in Patagonia, Argentina, and saw firsthand how a country's economy and currency can suddenly collapse. Currency collapses frequently wiped his parents out financially, so he understood intuitively the fragility of the financial system and how quickly something can go from valuable to valueless. He would often tell a story of going to the supermarket with his mother in the mid-1980s during a major bout of hyperinflation. His mom held two bags of money, which both contained her weekly salary. They were in a race to grab as many items off the shelf before the store manager could reprice the items. You see, because of spiraling inflation, the actual money was barely worth the paper it was printed on, and prices for goods and services were constantly fluctuating. In such a scenario, the best course was not to hold on to money but rather spend it as soon as you possibly could. To save it was to lose it. To spend it was to use it.

This experience gave Wences a unique view into the core function of money and informed his sensibility about currencies and the role money should play in a society. His past, combined with work as a tech entrepreneur, gave him the ability to understand the intersection of connectivity, finance, and technology better than anyone. It made him the perfect ambassador for Bitcoin.

Handsome and self-assured, Wences was well-liked by other wealthy tech investors, and he moved easily among the Silicon Valley set. And it was through these relationships that Wences introduced some of the richest and most powerful investors to Bitcoin, earning him the unofficial title "patient zero" because he infected so many Silicon Valley billionaires with the Bitcoin bug – including Thiel, Reid Hoffman, and Chamath Palihapitiya, among others. Rumor has it he bought the coin for $3.

Briger and Wences met on a family ski trip at a lodge in the Canadian Rockies in January 2013. It was exactly the type of place you might imagine billionaires would vacation: a huge sprawling house in the mountain with private gyms, separate help quarters, high ceilings, and burning fireplaces in multiple rooms, illuminating through soft warm light large oversized dark leather couches and paintings and taxidermy on the walls. It was the type of light that makes everyone look good.

After a day of helicopter skiing, Briger, Wences, and the other guests retreated to an expansive living room and talked about the very thing that allowed them to enjoy this type of lavish life in the first place: investing.

When it came time for Wences to speak, he didn't talk about buying some obscure government bond that was being overlooked by the market. Nor did he talk about Apple or Facebook, which continued to make new highs that year as tech led the market higher. Instead, he talked about what was still an obscure type of new investment that to him solved a centuries-old problem with money: Bitcoin.

Wences first discovered the crypto coin in early 2011. He and a group of friends were planning a road trip on an old school bus when he received a call from his friend in Argentina. He needed $2000 to repair the bus, and Wences had to send the money right away. The problem was at the time Argentina had insanely strict capital controls. Wire transfers weren't really an option. Nor was Western Union. If you wanted to get cash into Argentina, you had to go through the Argentine Central Bank, a mind-numbingly arduous process that seemed too onerous for the relatively small amount of funds needed for the bus repairs.

One of Wences' friends suggested using this new type of digital currency called Bitcoin, which could send money to anyone, anywhere around the world, with no banking intermediary. This concept seemed suspect at best for Wences, a man who knew a thing or two about the fintech industry.

But with time tight and his friend in need of cash, Wences figured he'd give it a try. This was before PayPal or Coinbase, in the very infancy of Bitcoin. But as the story goes, Wences went on Craigslist and found someone willing to sell him $2000 worth of Bitcoin. At the time, Bitcoin was basically brand new, and acquiring it without mining it was difficult. Most transactions were actually done in person, with buyers and sellers exchanging flash drives with Bitcoin stored on them.

Wences and his Craigslist customer decided they would meet at an Internet cafe to make the exchange. When Wences arrived, he found himself sitting across from some wild-looking guy with thin, long white hair. He looked like a character from *Lord of the Rings*.

Wences gave the $2000 in cash, but before he did, the guy made Wences download an app and scan some QR code.

"We're done," the man said.

The whole process happened so fast that when Wences left the cafe, he thought for a second that he had been scammed. But a few hours later his friend from Argentina called.

"I got the Bitcoin! We're all good with the money. The bus should be ready. Can't wait to see you. Thank you!"

Wences was in disbelief.

But he was also something else. He was hooked. And at that moment, an obsession began. He read everything and talked to anyone he could about the space. He was fascinated by the prospect of a completely decentralized network that allowed users to exchange value for free. Best of all, because of how Bitcoin worked (more on that later), he felt 100% safe transacting over its network, called the *blockchain* (more on that, too). In fact, he even paid a group of hackers to try to find a security flaw in the system.

They found none.

"To me, Bitcoin is like the Internet in the early 1990s," Wences said.

At first the analogy seems strange. How do you compare a newly created digital coin of vague origins to the sprawling reach of the Internet? But to Wences, Bitcoin and the blockchain were the other half of the Internet. It was the money part of the Internet. Imagine if you could extend all the powers of the Internet to the properties of money and digital gold. This was a profound statement coming from the man who was widely credited with launching the Internet in Argentina and who was also at the fore of many fintech enterprises, including Banco Lemon, which provided financial services to the unbanked in Brazil.

You have to remember what the Internet looked like in the mid-1990s. It was very rudimentary. The browsers were clunky. You had to literally call into the Internet using a landline phone. The connection was slow. Downloading pictures often failed. Watching video was almost impossible unless you had the best of connections, and even then it was pixelated and unreliable. The only thing the Internet was really good for was email and reading the latest stories online. But despite its limited capabilities, the early Internet was already a disruptive force that disintermediated a lot of traditional businesses and institutions.

First-class mail volume for the post office peaked in 2000 with 103 526 pieces. It has declined each year since to the point where last year's total was the same as it was in 1969. And that's just the start.

In 2000, estimated advertising revenue for the newspaper industry was $50 billion, and circulation for all newspapers touched 80 million, according to Pew Research. Today, those figures almost seem like a fantasy. Advertising is around $10 billion, and total circulation is around 20 million. People moved online. There is no need to get a physical newspaper when you can get the same article faster by looking at your phone. The industry has become, as Peter Diamandis would say, digitized and dematerialized, and ultimately demonetized.

That process caught the attention of investors and gave rise to the first dotcom era. Now, the interesting thing about the dotcom boom of the 1990s is that it was both a bubble and ultimately not a bubble. Amazon launched in 1994 as a way to sell books, which to the Barnes & Noble faithful seemed ridiculous. In fact, Barnes & Noble chairman Leonard Riggio said he would one day "crush" Amazon. But founder Jeff Bezos saw that the Internet was growing 2300% a year, and he knew people liked to buy books. And when the company went public in 1997, it was an instant hit with investors, even if the company was still losing money. Did investors get ahead of themselves? Yes, of course. So, when

Amazon shares, like those of many high-flying tech companies of the late 1990s, eventually crashed in 2000, losing at one point 90% of its value, many traditional investors could hardly contain their schadenfreude. Even Bank of America, which had a "Buy" rating on the company, urged investors to avoid the stock citing in part valuations and slowing holiday shopping season due to the crashing stock market.

What so many at the time missed is that Amazon wasn't about delivering books. Its value wasn't tied to the ups and downs of the holiday season. Amazon was about disruption. Bezos would famously say "Your margin is my opportunity," and what he meant by that is that Amazon could become the world's most efficient retailer, cutting out middlemen and giving its customers everything from food, entertainment, books, furniture, air conditioners – whatever you wanted – and could get it to you in two days or less.

Now, in 1994 it was almost impossible to forecast the disruptive power of the Internet. But 30 years later, the Internet is at the center of everything you do. We watch high-definition videos. We bank. We trade stocks. We send videos and complex images in the blink of an eye. We shop for everything from food to automobiles, and we do so by using a half-pound device that fits snugly into our pocket. The moral of the story is that it's hard to price any early-stage asset that's based on a new technology. Whether it's Apple, Amazon, Google – you pick the company – the early-adoption cycle is always volatile, and as a result, prices for those assets often soar, crash, and eventually soar again as they redefine and create new industries.

Bitcoin is following that path. It's like all the other early new technologies. You have early adopters, almost cult-like devotees. They're the first people to use cell phones. They're the people on the mountain in the 1980s channeling their inner Gordon Gekko, screaming into a brick phone. But the brick gets smaller. It begins to fold. It offers more capability as more people join the network. Before you know it, everyone has a cell phone. Why? Because it's easier and more convenient than a landline, even though that landline worked just fine for 50 years. Imagine living without a cell phone today.

And of course, once the hype cycle breaks, the stock crash, critics in unison say "I told you so," but something else happens. The technology gets better. More people are starting to use Amazon. Before you know it this new technology takes off, and everyone is left to wonder "How did that happen? How did I miss it? It was so obvious."

What always struck Wences as odd is that many of the original Amazon investors bailed on the company before it really achieved its dominance.

"The interesting thing was that many of the insiders who own Amazon pre-IPO sold, other than the founder," said Wences. "And that's often the case with disruptive technologies. You look at the trajectory of many tech companies and many of the people involved sell too early. They haven't been drawing a salary and want to get paid. Maybe they're relieved they made some money and can't see the full potential. And I think the same thing is happening here with Bitcoin."

It sparked a curiosity that soon turned into a passion for Briger and later became a series of sizable investments.

Years later, sitting atop a paddleboard in the Pacific, Messing would also contract the Bitcoin fever.

"The interesting thing is, if Briger had been some Silicon Valley tech bro, I would've totally ignored everything," said Messing.

Why Bitcoin?

To me, Bitcoin represents what happens when you combine the transformative power of the Internet and mash it together with the immutable power of value in all forms. This is the Internet of money. This is a traffic system that moves at the speed of light and processes transactions in a completely unhackable way. It's decentralized, where trust and verification are a shared responsibility. Bitcoin and blockchain could do for money what the telegraph did for information. When the telegraph was invented, it radically changed how information was transferred and gave rise to whole new industries. But you couldn't move money with a telegraph. Money was still physically transported.

Now, you might be thinking, "Mooch, take it easy. We've had digital money for years. Western Union has been around since the 1800s. I can Venmo my friends digital cash on my phone!"

That's all true, but those are point-to-point closed networks that exist inside the financial edifice. They are completely regulated and controlled by governing bodies all over the world. Bitcoin is decentralized. It exists outside that construct using a program that is so simple and so brilliant (more on that later) that it will forever change the financial world. Bitcoin is not controlled by any government entity. It does not require a bank to transact. It has become increasingly part of the financial system but still remains wholly independent. You can take your Bitcoin off the grid and complete everyday transactions.

It is the first global currency not issued by a central bank or government authority and controlled entirely by the people. This is a quantum leap in the history of money. In some ways, it fulfills the original promise of currency of being able to transact and store value. This is an important point. Every currency around the world is issued by a country's central bank and is backed by the full faith and credit of that government. If you go to Europe, you have to take your dollars, which are issued by the Federal Reserve, and exchange them for euros, which are issued by the European Central Bank. To regulate their respective economies, those central banks will control the amount of money in circulation. Since the Great Financial Crisis of 2008 central banks around the world have been in overdrive to print as much money as they can to literally try to print their economies back to life.

This has acted as a silent tax on citizens. As more money goes into circulation, that currency becomes less valuable. It's simple supply and demand. The more there is of one particular object, the less valuable that object becomes. As a result, central bank money printing, once a relatively obscure topic debated among academics and economists, has now gone mainstream. People who would otherwise never care about the Fed policy started protesting. Remember the Tea Party? It was all a rejection of what some considered to be a moral hazard enabling a rigged system, with the average mom and pop picking up the tab in the form of higher inflation.

The roots can be traced to the enormous bailout packages the government gave to the big banks after they all but collapsed during the mortgage crisis in 2008. Advancements in financial engineering allowed more Americans to access mortgages. Generally speaking, this is a good thing, as home ownership is the path to the American Dream. Everyone was making money in housing. Homeowners were getting rich. Banks were making money. And the government had created a whole new market for mortgage debt. But Wall

Street being Wall Street, many banks decided to extend riskier mortgages to people who really couldn't afford them. Everything was fine until one day those same people couldn't make their payments and the whole system collapsed. Faced with a once-in-a-generation crisis, policymakers had two choices: let the banks fail and allow the US economy to descend into a second Great Depression or embark on the greatest experiment on fiscal policy central banks have ever tried. We chose the latter and embarked on an unprecedented effort to stimulate the financial system by extending the Fed's balance sheet and printing trillions of dollars.

It preserved the financial system, but at the cost of tacitly endorsing reckless behavior. As many in the public saw it, banks could take outsized financial risks, to the benefit of people who ran them, and the United States would be there to clean up the mess if everything exploded. No one who ran a major financial institution involved in the mortgage crisis ever was charged with a crime.

Suddenly, there was a populist movement against Wall Street. People who had never protested before were taking to the streets in the "Occupy Wall Street" movement, in an effort to "stop the fat cats." People worried the Fed's actions would save the super-rich and stick everyone else with the tab. They became the villain. In 2001, public trust in Alan Greenspan's Fed stood at 74%. By 2012, it had declined to 39%.

Out of that distrust and anger was borne an acceptance of an alternative. No one was even thinking about Bitcoin in the charged days of 2008–2010, but some disaffected factions were ready for something else, something outside the system, something that was truly theirs that could not be touched or diluted, or, in effect, taken from them to cover up the financial misdeeds of a select and powerful few, or so the thinking went.

To be fair, I was not in touch with this sentiment. I was more myopically focused on the health of my customers and the integrity of the financial system. I was aware of the anger in America and the resentment toward Wall Street. I understood that frustration, but candidly speaking, in the dark days of 2008 and 2009, I was more concerned about making payroll. Still, for the very first time, "regular" people grew disillusioned with the financial system they knew. They were open to an alternative that could operate within the existing system but also be distinctly outside of it.

When COVID shut down the world and central banks resorted to the same playbook they did in 2008, it was clear to me that more and more investors would seek out an alternative to fiat dollars. It made sense. It wasn't about a disagreement on monetary policy, or distance for fiscal largesse. After the fiscal and monetary response to the Great Financial Crisis and now COVID, seeking a hedge against debasement was fiduciary responsibility.

While logic and reason were behind me, shifting from a traditional asset manager to a Bitcoin fund was a major business and life decision. If this failed and Bitcoin flamed out, I'm not sure I would ever professionally recover. I would be the Wall Street guy who bought at the high, only to flame out.

But in thinking about the pivot, I recalled a conversation I had with Michael Saylor. He and I were going back and forth about Bitcoin. Saylor is a Bitcoin maximalist. In his mind, there is no better investment in the world.

Saylor is one of the great geniuses of our time. An MIT grad, he founded the software company MicroStrategy in the early 1990s, just before the Internet boom. His company was a dotcom darling, and he saw firsthand how quickly a boom can turn into a bust. His gray hair and short beard belied his youthful soul. In truth, Saylor is more than an entrepreneur; he's a futurist, and he knew how to profit from trends others could not see.

But unlike many Bitcoin enthusiasts, Saylor didn't start out as a bull. In fact, he was anything but, and in December 2013 he took to Twitter and torched the space:

#Bitcoin's days are numbered. It seems like a matter of time before it suffers the same fate as online gambling.

In fairness to Saylor, the early days of Bitcoin were uncertain and scary. Exchanges were often hacked; the regulatory framework was a disaster. It was an emerging phenomenon in cyberspace, but it was unclear whether it was a security or commodity. How would governments and regulators respond to Bitcoin's rise? No one knew.

But as time passed and Bitcoin only became more prominent and more valuable, Saylor realized that Bitcoin's resilience spoke to its enduring value. So did the fact that so many imitators had come along in the form of competing coins and had done little to dent Bitcoin's supremacy.

When we made our initial investment, I called Saylor.

"What is the one thing that makes Bitcoin go higher?" I asked him.

"Let me throw the question back at you," Saylor replied. "What is the one thing they can't make more of?"

The "they" he was referring to wasn't just one entity. It was everything: governments, corporations, citizens. Anything that could ruin value.

"Money?" He continued. "Governments print money all the time? Bonds? Never printed more."

Real estate?

To Saylor, there was nothing scarce about real estate. And he would often point out in subsequent speeches that coastlines, the most prized pieces of real estate due to their scarcity, always seem to get bigger.

"They're building all the time. Beachfront property? They just build more. Look at Dubai! A lot of man-made waterfront property. Look at Miami," Saylor would later say. "When they run out of room, they just build more. Ever fly over the middle of the country? There's nothing but land."

Neighborhoods can go bad. Hurricanes or other natural disasters can strike at any time. Maintenance and insurance eat up costs. To Saylor's point, it's not really scarce.

"Public companies have competition, tariff risk, execution risk. Government risk. Alibaba is a great company, until the Chinese government bans it. You stack all those risks up, and you get 7% a year," Saylor concluded, referencing the long-term average return for equities. Even dominant public companies faced challenges in the form of competition or technology. Xerox was a verb in the 1980s and 1990s. Now it's a punchline.

In his view, pretty much every investment had the chance of being diluted or mismanaged, except Bitcoin.

"Bitcoin has been copied 6000 times, and all those copies have failed. And now it's emerged at 95% of all the monetary energy in the crypto space. And to me, that says Bitcoin is Facebook, not Myspace."

Myspace was the wildly popular social network that preceded Facebook, or as it was called back in those early days, "The Facebook." Founded in 2003 by UCLA dropout and musician Tom Anderson, Myspace grew to become the biggest website in the world. It is hard to believe now, but it had more traffic than Google at the time. In 2005, Rupert Murdoch's New Corporation purchased it for $580 million. By 2007, 320 000 users were signing up for it a day. Its moat seemed pretty safe. It boosted an upstart tech culture backed by a legacy media billionaire and was growing like a weed. But News Corporation's culture choked the innovation out of the social media company, and soon after Anderson left, a new start-up called Facebook with a guy named Mark Zuckerberg at the helm soon overtook it. Zuckerberg wasn't interested in selling. He wanted to conquer social media and understood almost intuitively the importance of growing and maintaining the network effort. Without the network, the company was really nothing. That was Myspace.

"People understand it's not a currency. It's not a payment network," said Saylor. In his view Bitcoin wasn't even digital gold.

Bitcoin solved a myriad of issues that had plagued the financial service industry for centuries. And unlike any other asset class in the world, it was noncorruptible. You could never make more. It was truly scarce and in demand. It was the future of digital property, and it was only a matter of time before the Street got behind the trade and there was mass adoption.

In Saylor's view, the chaotic early days of crypto rid the market of many of the bad actors. The regulatory framework was clearer. Tax treatment was clear. There was even a growing consensus in the investment community about what Bitcoin really was.

"It's bigger than all of that. It's a bank in cyberspace that allows millions of people to store their money. Bitcoin has emerged from a casino gambling story to the savings account at the end of the universe."

The naysayers cited feelings; the believers cited facts, and the facts were simple: Bitcoin had crushed every other investment in the last 1-, 5-, and 10-years. At the end of 2020, it had returned more than 45 000% since its inception.

The future was staring us right in the face, and it was time to make a move. So instead of waiting for the future to disrupt us, my partners and I decided to disrupt ourselves. I called a meeting.

Chapter Five

The Coin Itself

WHILE THE ORIGINS OF blockchain technology are murky, with academic references to similar technologies dating back to the 1970s, most agree that Bitcoin can be traced to a person (or people) using the pseudonym Satoshi Nakamoto. Until October 31, 2008, no one had ever heard of Satoshi, but an eight page white paper supposedly authored by him was sent to a mailing list. Who is Nakamoto? No one knows. The paper contained only a link to the website http://bitcoin.com.

Some have suspected that Nakamoto is actually more than one person. Others believe Satoshi is a psychological operation (PSYOP) by the Central Intelligence Agency (CIA). Whoever or whatever he was, the paper produced a concept that was so revolutionary and brilliant that it changed money forever.

It gave birth to the modern concept, and popular understanding, of a digital token or "coin" along with the concepts of "blockchain" and "mining" – and explained how these three things work together to allow one party to transfer value to another without the need of an intermediary. The paper proposed doing so by explicitly operating outside the traditional financial system and without government oversight. It explained how two parties could exchange value without exchanging a physical good and without using a bank or government entity.

This was a radical concept. Digital money has existed for a while, but it's always been on closed-circuit end-to-end networks. Products like DigiCash and ECash existed in the early 1990s as forms of payment that eluded the established financial system. But those products were centralized and relied on the network to confirm transactions. Bitcoin was completely decentralized. Its network was composed of disparate parties who were both users of the network but also, more importantly, custodians of it, too.

Bitcoin transactions would be recorded on a digital distributed ledger called a *blockchain*. Anyone with an Internet connection and access to computing power and energy could choose to participate in a process to record and verify those transactions, called *mining*, and/or receive a copy of the ledger that process produced, called a *node*. Those users who chose to mine Bitcoin, meaning those with the technical know-how and specialized equipment, could solve complicated math problems using, effectively, a sophisticated version of random guessing and be rewarded with fees paid in Bitcoin. By solving these increasingly complex math problems, Bitcoin miners maintain the trust and integrity of the ledger and ensure no one can double-spend the same Bitcoin. To incentivize this legion of independent workers, Nakamoto's paper said that anyone who can verify 1 megabyte (MB) worth of Bitcoin transaction would be rewarded with part of a Bitcoin. But Bitcoin miners do more than just verify transactions. They represent the decentralized trust that is crucial to upholding the Bitcoin ecosystem, and in doing so, they uphold the legitimacy of Bitcoin transactions by authenticating each one.

Individual transactions (for example, one person sending some Bitcoin to another person) are bundled into blocks and then added to a chain of blocks (i.e. a "block chain"). To confirm a block, a Bitcoin miner must solve this series of complex math problems before other miners do. Specifically, they have to solve for the correct 64-digit hexadecimal number called a *hash*. Because hashes are so unique, they are hard to replicate. This process of confirming and validating transactions is referred to as *proof of work*. You can think of it as a virtuous cycle where the ledger, or blockchain, is maintained by miners, who are in turn rewarded in tokens (in this case Bitcoin).

In a lot of ways, the Bitcoin mining process is analogous to gold mining; it gets harder over time, and manufactured scarcity should cause the price of Bitcoin to increase over time. Nakamoto specifically designed it this way, when he created the original Bitcoin protocol by ensuring only 21 million Bitcoin would ever be created. That's it. That's all there can ever be. And that scarcity is what imbues Bitcoin with value. Unlike most governments, which can and have been printing money like it's going out of style, Bitcoin miners can't only print more than 21 million Bitcoin. In a way, all the Bitcoin that have ever been created already exist – all you can do is mine to release them, and that process is designed to become more difficult over time. In fact, the reward for mining Bitcoin is cut in half every time 210 000 blocks are mined, a process referred to as *halving*. Making it harder to mine Bitcoin preserves its scarcity.

If we suddenly realized we had more gold than we thought existed, gold would get cheaper. Similarly, if gold mining became easier or cheaper over time, that would drive down the price of gold. The notion of mining vast amounts of precious metals like gold from asteroids is somewhat poorly thought through, as even if it were technically possible to mine vast quantities of gold from an asteroid, the result would be to flood the gold market with a trillion dollars' worth of gold, which would likely lead to a crash in gold prices. Supply and demand.

That's a lot, so let's break this down in a simpler way.

If I wanted to send you $100, I could go on my phone, log into my bank, and send money from my account to yours. Your bank trusts that my bank knows how much I have in my account. In other words, I'm good for the money. Then, our banks get to work – mine debits $100 from my account and sends the message to your bank, which credits $100 to yours. In addition to the two banks being involved, there were middlemen who helped the banks communicate and validate those amounts, as well as ensure everyone involved is a good actor. If the transfer is cross-border, it's likely those banks need even more intermediaries – all to simply create a ledger of accounts and make sure I, in fact, have $100 to send. In exchange for helping with this transfer, a fee (or more precisely, fees) are applied to pay all the intermediaries that made that transaction work. Those fees can add up, and the process can take a lot of time (days, even weeks).

Blockchain removes those middlemen by outsourcing that process of confirming and verifying the transaction to the miners. Then, the nodes making up the ledger that keeps track of all transactions are maintained by a distributed global system of voluntary participants. Each transaction is recorded in a block, and when you add a bunch of those transactions or blocks together, a chain is created, and that is the blockchain. The blockchain is continuously verified and updated by the miners, and a copy is sent to everyone running a node.

Satoshi's paper did something else especially important; it solved for double-spending. People have been trying to create digital money since the term *digital* was invented. The problem with many early digital currencies is that since it was digital, it was also easy to copy, and unscrupulous people could effectively spend twice on the same purchase. But because of cryptography and the blockchain, the miners verify all those transactions and the block. This was a huge breakthrough because, prior to the paper, no one had really figured out how to make a digital currency that couldn't be double-counted.

Now, some of you might be thinking, what is all this stuff? It sounds like mental gymnastics with a touch of math. But there's a simple analogy I like to use to describe this ecosystem.

You can think of blockchains as businesses. If they are a good idea, with efficient execution and customers like them – just like physical businesses – people will want to use their product. However, for on-chain businesses, to access their ecosystem, you will likely need to purchase/earn and use their native tokens/coins. This concept shouldn't be too difficult to understand, as you've probably done it before. When you go to Las Vegas, you exchange government-issued fiat dollars for chips, which are then used at the poker or blackjack tables. Those chips are like a tokens; they allow you to gamble and have more efficient access to the economy of the casino. But they do something else. They also allow the casino to, in theory, operate more efficiently, as managing cash is tricky and filled with regulatory hurdles. Also, since those chips work only in the casino where issued, this helps the casino minimize fraud. For example, a gambler who has just lost a bet might try to grab their cash off the table and run away. But if the money being gambled is in the form of chips rather than cash, this bad actor will still have to deal with the casino again to exchange those chips for cash. If all you do is take chips, the casino doesn't really care, because they already have your money. Finally, the system helps create customer loyalty; casino customers using the same chips and sharing in the customer experience creates a community around that specific casino brand.

In this scenario, the customer enters the casino, takes US dollars and exchanges it for a chip that they can use to gamble. That chip (ideally lots and lots of them) can then be turned back into dollars when the person decides to "cash out" and leave the casino. At each step of the way, those transactions are verified, from the initial exchange of the dollar into the chip to the wagering of that chip on a particular game to ultimately the exchanging of that chip back into dollars. Each step of the way, the process is checked and verified by the employees of the casino.

This is not that different from exchanging fiat currency into Bitcoin and then transacting with it using the blockchain. You take your dollars (or another currency), exchange it for Bitcoin, transact over the blockchain, and then if you want, can turn that Bitcoin back into dollars and leave. Each step of the way, the process is verified, checked, and confirmed by the miners on the Bitcoin network.

For many who believe in the future of on-chain businesses, the goal is to eventually not have to move back and forth between Bitcoin and fiat currencies. Eventually, they believe that the same tokens used to access these digital businesses will have value beyond that specific ecosystem and be used to buy and sell services and goods everywhere. For now, it is still necessary to transfer tokens like Bitcoin into fiat like US dollars to buy more goods and services – but even in that case, if the token is part of a system (like Bitcoin) that is highly valued, the costs of switching back and forth are considered worth it by millions of people.

And to me that's where the real promise is. Bitcoin is the Internet of money, but it represents so much more.

Bitcoin is the dematerialization and democratization of the ability to send value from one person to another, one entity to another. The Internet has allowed us to transmit images, information, and services seamlessly around the world. It's instant, almost magical in its scope and power. Before the Internet, you needed to find information in a physical book or documents. To send that information, you needed to buy a stamp, place a document in an envelope, and then mail that document. You hoped it reached its intended recipient. But the Internet dematerialized that process.

Bitcoin is the other half of the Internet. It is the digitization of physical money. And in an interconnected world where every human and every machine is seemingly connected, where there are trillions of sensors, Bitcoin is the future of value.

Digital currencies aren't exactly new, and chances are you've used them without really knowing it. Credit card points, which can be redeemed to buy a good and a service, are a type of digital currency. But credit card points and old technologies like eCash are centralized. They work only on a closed-end network. If that network disappears, those points or cash are worthless. But Bitcoin is a truly global currency. People all over the world are using Bitcoin to transfer and store their money.

But unlike other fiat currencies, there is a fixed supply of Bitcoins. No new Bitcoins can be created. There are only 21 million. That's it! That's all that will ever be created.

Now contrast that to what's happening with the US dollar. According to the Kobeissi Letter, since 2020, the

United States has printed nearly 80% of all dollars in circulation. At the start of 2020, there was $4 trillion in circulation. Now there is nearly $20 trillion. It's a staggering sum. Now, you might be thinking, "Wow, more money in my pocket – sweet!" But remember what would happen if we brought back a rocket ship full of gold? The problem is each time the Fed prints more money, each dollar becomes increasingly less valuable as there are more dollars floating around. And if you're wondering why things are costing so much around the world, it's because central banks have been printing money like it's going out of style.

But best of all, Bitcoin is completely portable. You can transport $1 worth of Bitcoin, or a billion dollars' worth, on a simple flash drive. If you live in a country where the banking system is fragile, inflation is eating up your savings. But with Bitcoin, you're immune from that inflation; you can keep all your money on a phone, and you can transact peer to peer without the government tracking you.

This offers profound advantages to every person along the socioeconomic scale. If you're living in a country where the government is unstable, where the value of the local currency can rise or fall 20% or more, Bitcoin offers much-needed stability. Those of us in developed countries take for granted the luxury of living with a stable currency. But in many places, political instability has given rise to monetary instability, and the value of a currency can collapse overnight.

This is happening right now in sub-Saharan Africa, where Bitcoin transactions are increasingly seen as a solution to runaway inflation. For these residents, crypto is a better store of value than its own currency. In Ghana, inflation has been out of control for years, recently reaching 25% in April 2024. That means every month, the value of a citizen's savings loses a quarter of its value. In such a scenario, spending, not saving, is the wisest course of action. The problem got so bad, the government tried to introduce another type of currency. But those efforts only created more confusion and problems among the population. With no relief in sight, many Ghanaians have decided to abandon their local currency altogether and take their chances with Bitcoin, which, while volatile, is still infinitely more stable, more portable, and more widely accepted than their local failing currency.

Bitcoin is also a solution for the unbanked. In Ghana, 40% of the population is unbanked, meaning its citizens don't hold a checking or savings account. And why would they? If the economy is in such disarray, it's only a matter of time before financial institutions like banks or credit unions collapse. And when that happens, say goodbye to your savings. But with Bitcoin, your savings are right there on your phone, backed up in the cloud or on a thumb drive.

Now let's say you're on the total opposite end of the economic spectrum.

Imagine you're a billionaire who lives in one of these countries where people just disappear, where one day you wake up and you're hanging upside down until you fork over some money. If you live in one of these places, if you're lucky, you might get advanced warning of an hour to leave.

What do you do?

Banks are off-limits. The local government has already frozen those assets. Hard assets like real estate or art are also frozen. But with a simple thumb drive, you can put $500 million in your pocket and take it wherever you want.

Try transporting $500 million of anything – dollars, gold, or even art. It's impossible. Even putting $500 million in a bank presents a series of challenges. But because Bitcoin is more government-free than most asset classes, it's immutable, storable, and transportable. And, in a pinch, you can use it to transact on a one-to-one basis.

Now you may ask why this imaginary billionaire would risk putting $500 million in such a volatile asset. After all, Bitcoin can routinely lose 10–20% in a month or week. That's true, but even if this person were to lose that money on Bitcoin price fluctuations, that's still better than having the government take your assets. Do you think said billionaire in this example can simply sell a Picasso or a yacht on the run? You can't because while those assets are great stores of value, they're not portable or transportable.

And therein lies the universal appeal of Bitcoin.

- *It's valuable:* It cannot be debased through central bank printing since there are only 21 million coins that can ever be mined.
- *It's portable:* It weighs nothing because there is no mass and it's entirely virtual.
- *It's incorruptible:* The billions of people who comprise the Bitcoin network act to ensure its safety and reliability.

Whether you're rich, poor, or, like most of the world, somewhere in between, investors will always seek out those characteristics in a store of value or medium of exchange. And of course, those characteristics have become the defining characteristics for currencies that function best. Money in its current form is relatively new. But the idea of money probably goes as far back to when the first prehistoric person felt the urge to repay another for some deed. In some ways, that was the first "I owe you," or debit if you will. Eventually, that debit would be recorded on a ledger of sorts, and so began the crude system of money of account, which would count up deeds or actions. Anyone who's ever gotten a friend with a hard-to-score reservation at a hot restaurant might say we're still using this system.

Money of exchange came along much later, but still some 8000 years ago. This is where a complicated system of bartering took hold, and people would trade one good for another, using a ledger to record the transactions along the way. Eventually, coins came into play in a system that better resembles the one we have now.

Bitcoin combines all the classic elements that have defined money and even solves for some new ones, because more than anything, Bitcoin, like all forms of money, exemplifies what happens when you combine technology with belief.

Chapter Six

Money, Money, Money

~

"THIS IS THE BODY of Christ," said Father Dobsonas, as he handed me a plain wafer. I put it in my mouth and felt the paper-thin and slightly sweet substance dissolve in my mouth.

"This is the blood of Christ," said Father Dobsonas, handing me a shiny cup. I was immediately taken aback by the acrid sting of my first and very tiny sip of wine.

Applause.

I had done it. I completed my first communion at the age of eight, in front of my beaming parents at Saint Peter's Church in my hometown of Port Washington, New York.

But I had also done something else, even if I wasn't aware of it at that time. I had begun my first interaction with money.

Aunts, uncles, friends, and neighbors showed me what felt like a small fortune. Checks for $10. Crisp five-dollar bills in white envelopes. All told I had $42. The very next day, my grandfather, Augustine DeFeo, took me to the local First Federal Savings and Loan to open a passbook savings account, which were accounts that allowed customers to keep track of deposits and withdrawals on a little book.

"Deposit $13, because that's my lucky number," he said to me. "But keep the rest," which I did, and quickly ran to the local toy store to buy G.I. Joe action figures.

It ignited a love affair with money that would never leave me – through my journey from a middle-class family from Long Island to the top of Wall Street to the next great transformative technology of our time: Bitcoin.

Back in the 1970s, savings accounts were paying 8–9%, and the experience of watching my dollars grow, seemingly out of thin air, thrilled me. At the time, money was different. It was physical. You completed a task and were rewarded with a physical note. Sometimes that bill was crumpled and smelled of a million sweaty hands. Sometimes it was crisp, fresh from the mint with a slight soapy and metallic odor.

But no matter its form, its purpose never changed: it was as it is now, a medium of exchange and a store of value, underpinned by a belief system that each bill represents a reward for a certain amount of work. By itself, each bill should have the same value as the next. The only difference between a $1 and $20 bill is the name of the president. But a Jackson is 20 times more valuable than a Washington not because of some inherent difference between the two bills, but rather the belief system that underpins their value. A two-dollar bill is good for a slice of pizza. A five-dollar bill is good for two slices and a Coke, even though those two bills are essentially identical, with the exception of the number printed on it.

My paper route in 1970s Long Island was good for a Hamilton per week. My First Communion was worth $42 in one day. While the metrics were not exactly uniform, the meaning was crystal clear. Money is the recognition or reward for an action, a service, or a good, and it's underpinned by a common belief system and a technology that allows all that to happen. From early seashells to coins to Western Union to, alas, Bitcoin, money is what happens when you combine belief and technology.

While you can feel and hold dollars in your hand, money has always been to some extent imaginary. After all, paper is paper. A $100 bill in the United States can buy you a very nice meal, but good luck getting steak in Paris with that same bill. To make that transaction work, you'd need to change those dollars into euros, minus the bank fee for the exchange.

What imbues money with value is the common understanding between two parties of a shared agreement of "worth." A good or service is worth a reward. Before there were physical coins or objects to trade, people would trade or barter for goods. For example, if you were an ancient farmer living in Mesopotamia in 6000 BCE, you might give someone two chickens for a new spear. As you can imagine, hammering out the exact details of the chicken-for-weapon swap required a tremendous amount of bargaining, and maybe even some threats. Complicating matters further, let's say one of those chickens dies, and the hunter who sold the spear now wants another chicken as compensation. Keeping track of this back-and-forth of who owes what to whom, to say nothing of the other transactions with other people, was incredibly inefficient and time-consuming. Still, it endured for thousands of years, until around 3000 BCE when people started to use clay tablets to record those transactions.

If one farmer paid two chickens to the warrior for the new spear, that transaction would be noted on a tablet or ledger, and by recording that trade, a standard unit was created. But something else happened. A store of value was created. The farmer was now able to record or store up prior deeds. So in this case, if he gave him two more chickens but received no spear, he would be owed a spear in the future that he could cash in at some point.

And as long as everyone trusts that they will make good on their debits, this system can continue to work. And this is the heart of money: a collective and mutually agreed upon value system. The hunter and the warrior have agreed to a common value (two chickens equals one spear), and they have a record of that transaction.

But what if you wanted to transact off that clay tablet with a third or fourth party? What if the hunter wanted to trade his sword for 10 bushels of wheat? He'd need a separate ledger to keep track of that transaction.

Enter physical money.

Around 3000 BCE, in what is now the Middle East, early evidence of physical money started to emerge, initially in the form of common objects like rice grains and shells. Over time, rare objects whose supply could be controlled started to be used for transactions. Mother of pearl and cowry shells were used in the Americas, Asia, and Africa. Eventually, metals entered the picture, and around 700 BCE the first evidence of government-issued coins started in the area that is now modern-day Turkey and China. The Lydia stater, named after the ancient Kingdom of Lydia, is widely considered to be the first coin, and it was composed of stamped gold and silver coins that were paid to military members as a form of salary.

This was a significant step and was made possible only by profound leaps in technology at that time. Making coins required people to know how to find the metals, in this case, gold and silver, and how to shape them into unified coins that could be used for compensation.

But the manufacturing of the coins themselves also represented a significant technological challenge. With coins, people could be compensated with a uniform measure of value that could be used as a means of transaction or a store of value. Most important, it was portable and durable. You could take your money with you and store it. No ledgers, animals, or objects. They were just simple coins that could be carried with you. Chickens, after all, have a very short shelf life, and carrying them around was cumbersome at best. And they lose all value when they die. But with the advent of coins, people could now move money around and transact peer-to-peer, without using a ledger, and still procure the items they needed.

And as long as people continued to have faith that those gold coins had value, the system could be sustained. And to ensure that faith, governments would stamp an official seal on the coin to ensure its purity. To prevent people from shaving off parts of the coins, they put ridges on the side. What these tiny details really represent is the very first introduction of technology, albeit primitive, to early systems of money. You can think of it in today's terms as the holograms that grace 100-dollar bills.

Even the material that the coins were made of – gold – required a shared faith. After all, what is gold? Pharoahs would line their tombs with it. Queens would dress in it. But curiously enough, there is another ancient element that is nearly identical to gold but worth far less: lead.

The two look, feel, and weigh about the same. In fact, they sit just protons apart on the periodic chart of elements, but one is basically worthless, and the other is hoarded by central banks around the world.

One is invaluable, the other basically valueless.

But why? After all, there are far more real-life use cases for lead than gold.

The answer to that question explains more than just the vagaries of various materials. The answer explains the secret of money. In the end, it's just the combination of belief and technology.

But while coinage as a commodity provided great benefits to ordinary citizens, it provided maybe something more valuable to governments: control. Political leaders could for the first time determine how much money circulated in the population, and they could also determine how that money was used.

While coins were easier to carry than cattle and chickens, they were still heavy, and storing and transporting large quantities was difficult. To get around this, merchants would issue paper receipts for large quantities of coins – the first IOUs if you will. And around the eleventh century, during the Song Dynasty in China, the first government-issued paper money was created. It reduced the heavy load of coins as international trade heated up, and it also solved for the difficulty of mining copper. Those papers were backed by gold, silver, or other metals, and doing so embedded them with value beyond the physical paper it was printed on. The paper effectively functioned as an IOU, which is how paper money functioned for centuries to come. And this represented a quantum leap in terms of how people interacted with money. The paper was in fact worth more than the paper it was printed on because people knew or believed that something more valuable and tangible was behind it – gold or silver – and that they could access those more valuable materials through the paper.

The problem with paper is that it is easier to counterfeit since the barrier to production is lower than mining and smelting rare materials. Still, the use of paper marks a crucial inflection point in the evolution of money as it is the best example of how a belief system can imbue value in a currency. Instead of a shiny and widely sought after and scarce metal, people are now willing to accept paper, or representative money, because of its convenience and efficiency.

This is a key point: the use of paper money highlights the connection between technology and faith that all forms of money possess. The greater the faith in the institutions backing the currency, the more valuable that money becomes. Eventually, users won't need to redeem their paper money for the physical asset backing it, because they know that the paper is just as useful in procuring goods and services. But this faith would be tested. The problem with paper money is that it's easy to create, which can be a great temptation to a government in need of cash and looking to stimulate its economy. And that's exactly what happened in thirteenth-century China. During the Yuan Dynasty, the first fiat money was issued. It wasn't backed by gold or silver, just the explicit promise that if you tried to counterfeit it or not accept it, you would be killed. I suppose that's one way to get people to accept your currency. But war created fiscal pressures, and to solve that, the government began to print more and more money. But the flood of new money only made the fiscal pressures worse as each unit was devalued, eventually leading to a loss of faith and citizens refusing to accept it. Eventually a new currency, backed by gold, was reintroduced, but the lesson was clear. Money exists in a delicate balance of faith, trust, and order, and if you disrupt any of those elements, chaos can ensue.

Prior to the Civil War, money in the United States was issued by private banks in various regions. This created an unruly and unstable system where one day a currency could collapse if its issuing bank went out of business. It wasn't until after the Civil War that the US government instituted a monetary system where banks could issue paper notes that were backed by government bonds. Still, the US monetary system was fragile, and confidence in bank notes was weak, leading to frequent bank runs. Following a particularly bad banking panic in 1907, the Federal Reserve, or Fed, was created in 1913 with the express purpose of imparting financial stability to the US monetary system. The Fed would control interest rates, supervise banks, and maintain financial order. Citizens could have more confidence in their money if they knew that it was ultimately backed by the government, which, theoretically, could never go out of business like a bank.

Back then, US dollars were backed by gold, a policy known as the *gold standard*, which was employed by many countries. The policy linked paper money to something physical, but it did something else: it prevented governments, or in this case central banks, from printing too much money since each dollar was backed by gold. If you wanted to print more paper, you needed to find more gold.

The policy may have led to stability, but it also prevented the US government from stimulating its economy, particularly during economic downturns, when central banks want to inject more money and liquidity into a slowing or stagnant financial system. During the Great Depression, the gold standard was suspended to allow the Fed to print more money to stimulate growth. After World War II, world leaders convened at the Mount Washington Hotel in Bretton Woods New Hampshire with the hopes of establishing a new financial world order. The world's leading economies agreed to go back on the gold standard, with all currencies by some measure backed by gold, in hopes of establishing a new economic world order. The dollar would be pegged to gold at $35 an ounce. Other central banks could exchange dollars for gold, making a dollar, for all intents and purposes as good as gold. The explicit promise of gold would hold everything together and ensure the public had confidence in the currency. The gold standard created a more predictable global economy, with the dollar becoming the world's reserve currency. Prosperity soon followed, and eventually everyone wanted dollars, making the dollar strong relative to other currencies and slowing exports.

In 1971, Nixon suddenly took the United States off the gold standard. In his view, doing so gave the Fed more flexibility. Surging inflation and a stagnating economy made sticking with the gold standard untenable. Exacerbating the situation, military spending and foreign aid were putting pressure on the US government's balance sheet, making dollars less attractive. If foreign holders decided one day to exchange their dollars for gold, the US government could face a gold run and potential loss of confidence in the government's ability to make good on its payments.

But if the US dollar wasn't backed by gold, what was it backed by? Why would investors want to hold paper if there was no gold attached to it? The answer was both simple and complicated. The dollar was no longer backed by gold, but it was backed by something even better: innovation. The United States still had the world's greatest economy, because it had the world's most innovative companies. IBM. General Electric. Goodyear Tire. Exxon. If you wanted to buy these companies, you needed dollars. If you want a piece of American ingenuity, you need American dollars. Gold would no longer determine what a dollar was worth. Demand would. The free market would, backed of course by the full faith and credit of the US government, the most powerful in the world.

But abandoning the gold standard did something else for the economy. It changed America's role in the world. In the 50+ years since America ditched the gold standard, the dollar is still the world's dominant currency, and that's because we have the world's most dominant and dynamic corporations, industries, and products. We're able to finance our deficits because we have the world's most innovative economy. This has acted as a double-edged sword. On one hand, we can print money we don't have because global demand for dollars is still great. This allows us to avoid depressions in times of economic duress, like the Great Financial Crisis or COVID. But if we print too much, we run the risk that investors will lose confidence in our currency and our ability to repay our debts.

And that is the key to any financial system or payment type. You need to have faith that the money you are receiving will have value. That's why gold played an essential role for centuries for different currencies around the world. It was meant to imbue worthless paper with the promise of value. It preserved the trust between a citizen and its government and ensured that a government could never abuse that trust by printing too much money. After all, gold is a rather imperfect currency. It's hard to take a bar to your local Walmart and shave some off to buy toilet paper. But a financial system that is trusted is limitless in its scope and power. And it is that leap of faith that allows me to walk into the Hunt and Fish Club, order a steak, and pay with it using a plastic card. We've moved from gold to paper to plastic to nothing physical at all, just a series of ones and zeros.

Bitcoin represents just the latest example in the constant evolution of money. And as with any evolution, its latest form solves for previous defects. Coins solved the hassle of carrying around ledgers and the coincidence of wants. Paper solved for the weight of coins, making it easier to transport. And Bitcoin has solved central bank debasements by limiting the number of coins that can be mined (also, it's way easier to transport).

But whatever form money has taken through time, a clear pattern emerges, and it's something economist and early Bitcoin backer and author Vijay Boyapati describes in four distinct stages in his must-read book, *The Bullish Case for Bitcoin*.

Collectables: This is the first stage, and it consists of objects that people desire. These include shells, beads, gold, and the like.

Store of value: Once enough people demand these objects, they will be recognized as a store of value over time. And as more and more people accept it as a store of value, that object's purchasing power will increase as demand drives up the price.

Medium of exchange: With steady purchasing power, the opportunity costs of using money to complete a transaction will diminish to a level where it is suitable for a medium of exchange. In other words, as more and more people use a particular currency, the value of that currency unit stabilizes, and people will feel more comfortable using it to purchase goods and services.

Unit of account: As money becomes more widely used as a medium of exchange, goods will increasingly be priced in terms of it. In other words, there are lots of items you can purchase using Bitcoin. But those items are usually based on the conversion rate from dollars to Bitcoin. For Bitcoin to be a unit of account, it will need to be accepted regardless of what the dollar conversion rate is.

In Boyapati's view, Bitcoin has firmly moved from the first stage to the second but has yet to fully move to the others, beyond of course, some novel examples. Bitcoin is still too volatile to make the everyday buying and selling of goods practical. But that is increasingly changing, particularly among the unbanked or those living in countries with increasingly unstable monetary systems. It may be a while before Bitcoin becomes a unit of account, particularly in countries that enjoy a stable financial system, but it's not inconceivable that we could see it in our lifetime.

Chapter Seven

The Pivot

THE PLAN WAS RELATIVELY simple. We were going to announce to the world through various media outlets that SkyBridge, our fund-of-funds business that had been a staple on Wall Street for nearly two decades, was going to jump into the deep end of the Bitcoin pool. The fund would invest $25 million to get started and would open it to accredited investors. We charged a comparatively low 75-basis points, which was considerably less than what Greyscale's investment trust, which before exchange-traded funds (ETFs) was considered the industry standard for Bitcoin-linked funds, charged.

It was November 2021, so most of the partners at the firm were still remote. I'm not a fan of Zoom, generally speaking. It's impersonal. The lighting and audio can be tough. Poor Internet connections can cause people to pixelate and resemble a talking Picasso. But one thing I do like is it forces everyone to look right at you. And I could tell from their faces that my team was behind me on this one. It didn't take a lot of convincing, which spoke to their collective entrepreneurial spirit.

But then again, we had done our homework over the past couple years, and we felt 100% comfortable about our initial concerns in three key areas: scale, regulation, and storage.

Scale was crucial, probably the most important aspect in deciding to invest in Bitcoin. How big is the market? If a currency is used by only two people, it's not really much of a currency, or anything for that matter. Apple's real value is not so much that they make a remarkable phone. It's the fact that there are more than a billion iPhone users around the world. They're all on the App Store, which makes those apps more valuable because there are more customers to serve. It's the network, the massive installed base of Apple users, that allows the superior iPhone technology to really distinguish itself.

When it comes to Bitcoin, that network effect is best captured by the number of wallets.

"Do we need to wait until Bitcoin reaches at least 100 million wallets?" I asked my partners.

Bitcoin wallets are essentially Bitcoin users. The greater the number of users, the more valuable Bitcoin would become. It represented adoptions. It was Metcalfe's laws in action. Robert Metcalfe was an engineer whose work laid the early foundations for the Internet in the 1970s. The son of a technician from Brooklyn, Metcalfe was fascinated by the idea that you could connect two computers and have them communicate with each other. He most famously developed a way to link computers while working at Xerox's Palo Alto Research Center and is widely credited with inventing Ethernet, the network technology that connects computers to online networks. He was so convinced of the power of connectivity that when Harvard refused to allow a first-year grad student to work on a potential computer network, he simply walked down the street and developed one at MIT. The interface message processor that he built for that project reportedly still hangs in his Boston home.

In his view, the value of a network is directly proportional to the number of parties engaged in that network. A fax machine that's only connected to another fax machine has limited value. But a network of fax machines, connecting millions of parties around the world, has great utility and value. One bank that is connected to one other has limited value to its customers. A bank that's connected to hundreds of other banks, connecting people who have money with people who need it, has unlimited value. Put simply, the greater the ability to connect with more people, the greater the value a particular network will have.

And that concept extends to Bitcoin as well.

The greater the number of wallets, the more participants on the Bitcoin network. Brett had already been doing months and months of research, and in his view, we didn't need to get to 100 million.

"80 million is enough," he said. "Bitcoin is already at $20,000. At the rate this thing is growing, we'll get to 100 million, possibly 300 million wallets in no time."

Problem one solved. The network was big enough and growing fast enough.

Problem two: regulation.

The crypto regulatory environment in 2020 was rapidly evolving and murky at best. It wasn't entirely clear where DC regulators and politicians stood when it came to Bitcoin and crypto generally. The pendulum swung between forward-thinking regulators like Securities and Exchange Chair Jay Clayton, who immediately recognized and welcomed sensible regulation around crypto, and his czar-like successor at the Securities Exchange Commission (SEC), Gary Gensler, who's done everything in his power to destroy it. And there was debate between the Commodity Futures

Trading Commission (CFTC) and the SEC about whether Bitcoin was a security or a commodity.

None of that really concerned me. For every Senator Elizabeth Warren who railed against Bitcoin, there was a Senator Cynthia Lummis there to defend it, and to some extent, the debate in Washington mirrored the hot debate raging on Wall Street and financial media.

What concerned me most about owning Bitcoin was government overreach. What was to stop a group of politicians or some government entity from ruling Bitcoin illegal and confiscating it?

"They can't," Brett said. "The IRS has already solved that."

In 2014, the Internal Revenue Service declared Bitcoin tangible property for tax purposes. It might seem strange to call Bitcoin property since it doesn't exist in physical form. You'll never hold a Bitcoin in your hand. It's entirely virtual. But the ruling provided a crucial protection.

Property rights in America are sacrosanct. One of the founding principles of the United States is the legal structure and protection of property rights. In fact, it precedes the founding of this country and dates all the way back to the Magna Carta, where no free man will be "dispossessed" of his property. Our Constitution guarantees that no person shall be deprived of property. That concept is the hallmark and anchor of our Anglo-American capitalist system. You can buy property in the United States, and you have title to that property, and the United States can't take that property from you without paying you for it. Even if they want to build an expressway through your house, they have to give you something for your property.

By classifying Bitcoin as property, the IRS basically assured investors that the government couldn't take your coins.

In short, no Czarist politician or bureaucrat was going to get their hands on my Bitcoin. How could they ban it? It was legally protected property. The courts would stop them. It was afforded all the same protection as any other property.

Problem two was checked off the list.

Of course, protecting Bitcoin from the government was one thing. Storing it was another, and that represented the last, albeit probably the easiest, hurdle to overcome.

Custody, or storing Bitcoin, has always been a thorny issue in the crypto world since the Mt. Gox hack in 2011. Mt. Gox was a crypto exchange that operated out of Tokyo from 2010 to 2014. At the time, it accounted for nearly three-quarters of all Bitcoin transactions. When it was hacked in 2011, thousands of Bitcoins were stolen, which sent shock waves through the industry and sent a chill down the spine of any investor thinking of buying Bitcoin. After all, if you couldn't trust the leading exchange to keep your Bitcoin safe, who could you trust? The exchange filed for bankruptcy in 2014, leaving a very black eye on the industry and a pall over Bitcoin prices in particular.

But over time, through increased investor interest, better and safer technology was established, and the more traditional Wall Street players entered the custodian business. Fidelity, Coinbase Prime, and New York Digital Investment Group all provided great custodian services, offering the same type of services as a traditional prime broker. The only difference was instead of processing, financing, and holding traditional assets like stocks and bonds, these clearinghouses of the new age were providing those very same services for Bitcoin.

The Street was obviously comfortable holding these assets. Maybe we should, too.

After years of research, we felt comfortable moving further into the world of crypto investing. And it wouldn't come a moment too soon.

Bitcoin was going to the moon.

COVID had turned the world upside down. But it also unleashed an unprecedented spree of global easing by central banks, which were desperate to avoid an economic collapse. The Fed and Congress were injecting trillions into the US economy. To keep the economy afloat, the government issued stimulus checks to millions of Americans, whether they needed them or not.

After a couple initial dark months at the onset of the pandemic, the economy exploded. With millions of Americans able to work from home, many companies not only survived the pandemic but thrived under it in ways no one thought possible. Technology was forcing the world to quickly move from the physical to the virtual, and Bitcoin was right at the center of it all. With central banks around the world furiously printing money, Bitcoin was having its moment. It went from $6000 before COVID to $30000 by the time we launched the fund.

Because we launched in the midst of a raging crypto bull market, the timing belied the serious and rigorous work that we had been doing the past two years. But that's alright. We were long-term believers, and if Bitcoin was top of mind for many investors, we figured that probably played into our hands.

It was time to get the message out: "To the Moon: SkyBridge Launches Its Bitcoin Fund."

The reaction to the initial press reaction was, to put it mildly, not particularly kind. Snarky, at times derisive. Pretty much every publication noted the 200%-plus run Bitcoin had had in 2020. A few couldn't help point to my 11-day stint as White House Communications director.

Whatever!

Had I bought Apple or even shares of Tesla, no one would've said anything. Heck, had I launched a special-purpose acquisition company (SPAC) no one would've said "boo." But financial media, much like the entities they cover, can be slow to spot changes and are often wary of new and untested technologies. They didn't understand Bitcoin. Many in the press took their cues from Warren Buffett and Charlie Munger, two of the greatest investors of all time, but also two people who never missed an opportunity to slam Bitcoin as a "zero" or liken it to a "venereal disease" or worse. "If Warren thinks it's a scam, well, it must darn right be a scam," the thinking went, all while Bitcoin continued its march higher. They would latch on to Jamie Dimon's "pet rock" comments.

And the colorful characters who populated the crypto landscape at the time, young arrogant guys with "Lambos" and Instagram feeds posting their Coinbase account returns, certainly rubbed some journalists the wrong way: "How could this be a serious investment? Look at who's buying! What could these kids HODLing and talking about their diamond hands and posting about their YOLO trades possibly know about serious finance?" It was easier to call it a scam than to do the hard work. But again, these are the same folks calling Amazon a bubble in 1999. If I've learned anything in my decades in finance, it's this: don't let the press manage your money.

So three days before Christmas in December 2020, I was about to go on CNBC and announce to the world we were starting our fund. I went on Scott Wapner's *Halftime Show*, which is CNBC's highest-rated broadcast and the one most popular with both institutional and retail investors alike.

I've known Wapner for years, having shared hundreds of dinners. He has one of the sharpest minds in all of financial journalism. But while being one of the nicest guys around, he's also no pushover, and his first question summed up the prevailing skepticism of the asset class and our move into it.

"Why now?" Scott asked in his dogged way. "You don't feel it's a little late? You don't feel that some investor may say, 'Well, now that SkyBridge has jumped into Bitcoin, that's got to be some type of top.'"

By the time we launched the fund, Bitcoin's price had already tripled that year, so his point was well taken. And it seemed every day, a new prominent investor was jumping into the deep end of the crypto pool, making our decision seem more a reaction to the hype as opposed to perhaps one that was helping drive it.

"It's early innings, Scott," I said. "We could be at the precursor of an avalanche of institutional investors wanting to put it on their balance sheet. Given the monetary situation, we feel there is a lot more room to run."

Three weeks later, we hosted a Zoom as a sort of broad outreach to every person in the SkyBridge network, which included both past and current clients, our salesforce, and anyone who ever attended one of our famous SALT events over the years. The goal was to lay out our thesis for getting involved. The turnout was so great that the call crashed due to overload.

People were fascinated by our move, even if they weren't necessarily in agreement with it. Client reaction was mixed and seemed to depend on one's role on Wall Street. Some called it mathematical blather. Some longtime clients liked it. The big banks, whom we relied on to distribute our product, were none too pleased. Why would they? We were now proponents of a new technology that could disrupt their business (they all came around). Morgan Stanley, which was our longtime distributor, wanted to impose limits on position sizes. Our fund was structured so that no single strategy could exceed 40%, and we didn't want a special exemption for Bitcoin.

But our timing could not have been better.

Chapter Eight

The Paul Tudor Jones Effect

———— ❧ ————

"For a long time, you were very skeptical of Bitcoin," said CNBC's Andrew Ross Sorkin. "But now that appears to have changed. What happened?"

It was May 11, 2020, and the great Paul Tudor Jones was on *Squawk Box*. The stock market had just hit a two-month high and had rallied 34% off the March lows when everyone was convinced the world was going to end. The world didn't end, but it was anything but normal. Schools and offices were closed. Many folks were still stuck at home. Sorkin, like many anchors at that time, was interviewing Tudor Jones from his home studio. After two of the most tumultuous months in American history, life was trying to get back to some semblance of normalcy. And one of the world's greatest investors was about to announce to the world that he was buying Bitcoin.

"Well, COVID happened, and the great monetary inflation happened," replied Tudor Jones. "And it made me begin to think about how you want to be positioned going forward."

He was of course referring to the trillions of dollars in COVID stimulus programs that the Fed and Congress approved to save the economy from another Great Depression. The Fed cut rates to near zero and rapidly expanded its balance sheet by injecting trillions of dollars into the crashing economy. Every type of program was announced to keep the credit markets from freezing. The Fed purchased more than $4 trillion in government securities to keep the bond markets from collapsing. But to keep the consumer alive, Congress and the Trump administration additionally passed more than $5 trillion in stimulus programs designed to keep the economy humming, including the Coronavirus Aid, Relief, and Economic Security Act, known as the CARES Act. This established the Paycheck Protection Program, or PPP loans, which help shuttered small businesses keep workers on their payrolls. It also provided for direct stimulus checks to be mailed out across the nation. The result was the biggest fiscal stimulus in US history. In fact, in the six months following COVID, the US government printed more money than in the previous 244 years.

The pandemic was a brutal and tragic event for the world, causing death and untold sorrow. But because of the massive stimulus programs, it was also, for many people, a financial boon. Many were working remotely and were saving on commuting costs. Restaurants and sporting events were closed, so people were saving more. Zooms and other work technologies not only allowed many companies to survive the pandemic, but it also helped them thrive. And as a result, consumers' fiscal health improved. According to Bank of America, customers who had between $1000 and $2000 before the pandemic had on average $4000 after it. Balances between $2000 and $5000 before the pandemic grew on average to $13 000.

Now you might be asking, where did all this money come from? Well, it's simple. The government did what it always does in times of trouble. It simply created more money by turning on the printing presses and transferred COVID's financial burden from the balance sheets of the private sector (consumers and business) to those of the public (government). At the start of the pandemic, the Fed's balance sheet stood at $4 trillion, up from $2 trillion following the Great Financial Crisis. After all the COVID spending, the Fed's balance sheet would more than double to nearly $9 trillion. Prior to COVID, total outstanding US debt stood at around $25 trillion. In 2010, it was just under $10 trillion, so this notion that we've been spending too much money for too long is not new. But COVID exacerbated that trend, and now the US government has $34 trillion in outstanding debt, and our debt to the gross domestic product (GDP) ratio now stands at a staggering 123% to GDP. These are dangerous and unsustainable numbers more appropriate for a developing nation, not the world's leading superpower.

This deluge of cash not only prevented the economy from falling off a cliff but also may have over-stimulated the economy. And Tudor Jones, like other smart investors at the time, knew that this was likely to cause major inflation when the economy eventually reopened.

"Just think about Bitcoin versus cash. When I think of stores of value, I think of it four ways: purchasing power, trustworthiness, liquidity, and portability. So, when it comes to trustworthiness, Bitcoin is 11 years old. There is very little trust in it. We're watching the birth of a store of value. And whether that's a success, only time will tell. What I do know is that every day that goes by, the trust in it goes up. If you take cash and you think about it from a purchasing power standpoint, if you own cash in the world today, you know your central bank has an avowed goal of depreciating its value 2% per year," Tudor Jones said. "So you have, in essence, a wasting asset in your hands."

In other words, nothing is free. If the government is going to debase its currency and create trillions of new dollars out of thin air, then the value of those dollars and related assets would likely fall. Investors need something outside the system, something that cannot be corrupted by fiscal and monetary largesse.

But Tudor Jones was also quick to note the other trends that were helping Bitcoin as well, namely, the push to move from the physical to virtual. In the summer of 2020, people were working over Teams and Zoom. They stopped going to movies and instead watched Netflix. They stopped going to grocery stores and instead opted for delivery services. Amazon Prime membership jumped. People were becoming more comfortable transacting on their phones and using cashless cash for transactions, a trend that Tudor Jones noted had been happening for years.

"My children don't carry cash. They barely even know what cash is," said Tudor Jones. "So we're clearly digitizing the global economy. We're getting into an increasingly more digitized world and Bitcoin will be that much more accessible by that universe of people that could own it. Every bull market has one common thread: an ever-expanding universe of people who own it."

And then he dropped the hammer, revealing that he had invested 2% of his portfolio in Bitcoin.

The importance of these facts cannot be understated. Tudor Jones is an investing legend and the pioneer of the modern-day hedge fund industry. He is considered among the greatest macro traders of all time, having famously cashed in on the Black Monday crash of 1987. His Tudor Investment Corp has managed more than $5 billion in assets. Tudor Jones had dabbled in Bitcoin in the past, but this was his most significant endorsement yet, and because he had such tremendous credibility on Wall Street, his investment gave cover to other asset managers to dabble in crypto, too.

"Paul Tudor Jones going on air provided a permission structure for asset managers to get involved in the space," Brett Messing would later say. "He's one of the most respected guys on Wall Street."

In subsequent interviews, Tudor Jones even likened buying Bitcoin to owning Apple in the 1980s.

"Now I know what it must be like to be a tech investor," said Tudor Jones. "It's like investing with Steve Jobs in Apple or investing in Google early. You have this group of people all over the world dedicated to seeing Bitcoin succeed in becoming a store of value. I've never had an inflation hedge with the kicker of having great intellectual capital behind it. I like Bitcoin even more now than I did then."

Of course, in 2020, Tudor Jones was just one of many investment legends to appear on financial media and *Squawk Box* in effusive praise of Bitcoin. In November, billionaire investor Stanley Druckenmiller appeared on CNBC and declared that he, too, owned the digital asset, mainly as a hedge against a declining dollar and said it could be a better investment than gold.

"Frankly, if the gold bet works, the Bitcoin bet will probably work better, because it's thinner, more liquid, and has a lot more beta to it," said Druckenmiller, who still noted that he owns many times more gold than Bitcoin.

"I'm a bit of a dinosaur, but I have warmed to the fact that Bitcoin could be an asset class that has a lot of attraction as a store of value."

Druckenmiller founded Duquesne Capital in 1980, one of the original and most successful hedge funds of all time. From 1981 to 2010, when he closed the fund, he returned on average 30% to clients. He managed money for George Soros and teamed up with Soros to break the Bank of England in 1992, betting on a severe decline in the pound that netted them more than a billion dollars in profit. He's a legend, not some new money hedge fund jumping in and out of the latest investment fad.

In the subsequent months, a who's who of hedge titans began adding Bitcoin to their portfolio. Dan Loeb, one of the smartest and most talented investors I know, revealed he took a stake in the digital asset after doing what he described as a "deep dive into crypto lately. It is a real test of being intellectually open to new and controversial ideas."

Soon more established asset managers entered the space. Rick Rieder, the ever curious and thoughtful chief investment officer from BlackRock, the world's biggest asset manager, went on *Squawk Box* and sang Bitcoin's praise.

"I think cryptocurrency is here to stay. I think it's durable. I think digital currencies and the receptivity – particularly millennials' receptivity – of technology and crypto assets is real," Rieder said. "I think Bitcoin is here to stay. I think it will take the place of gold to a large extent. It's a lot more functional than passing a bar of gold around."

Pretty soon, Bitcoin quotes were increasingly flashing on the TV screens, right beside quotes for the Dow and S&P 500. And it wasn't just Bitcoin. Prices for Ethereum and Solano jockeyed for position next to quotes for oil and the 10-year yield. Equity strategists were increasingly referencing Bitcoin in their views of the overall macro stock market.

But the biggest and most important endorsement was yet to come.

Chapter Nine

The Musk Man Giveth and Taketh

On December 20, 2020, an eye-opening exchange on Twitter caught many market participants' attention.

In the wee hours of the morning, Elon Musk, the richest man in the world and the chief executive officer (CEO) of Tesla and SpaceX among other companies, took to Twitter (he would later buy it and rename it X) and posted an image of a bearded monk trying to resist the temptations of a beautiful woman bent over a bed. It included the words, "Me trying to live a normal and productive life." The woman's rear end is covered with the word Bitcoin.

The post sent the price of the coin sharply higher and attracted the notice of Michael Saylor, the founder and CEO of MicroStrategy Inc. His company had recently put Bitcoin on its balance sheet.

"If you want to do your shareholders a $100 billion favor, convert the [Tesla] balance sheet from US dollars to Bitcoin," Saylor tweeted. "Other firms on the S&P 500 would follow your lead & in time it would grow to become a $ trillion favor."

"Are such transactions even possible?" Musk replied.

"Yes," Saylor replied. "I have purchased over $1.3 Billion in #BTC in the past months & would be happy to share my playbook with you offline."

Musk had tweeted about Bitcoin in the past, at times referring to it as his "safe word" and had even mocked Bitcoin as "almost as bs as fiat money" in a previous tweet. Musk's post came at 3:45 a.m. ET, so it wasn't entirely clear if he was serious or had been out late. Later that night, or morning, Musk took to Twitter again and posted, "One word: Doge."

That sent Dogecoin, a dog-theme cryptocurrency that had been around since 2013, surging 40%. Dogecoin had always been a joke. In fact, it was started by two software engineers as a way to mock what they saw as wild speculation in the crypto asset space. Unlike Bitcoin, Dogecoin is designed to be inflationary, spitting out new coins every

THE MUSK MAN GIVETH AND TAKETH [95]

minute. The official logo is the face of Kabosu, a Shiba Inu dog from Japan. The whole thing is intended to be a satire, and some interpreted Musk's tweeting about it as a shot to the crypto community. He capped off the evening, or morning, by tweeting, "come for the comments, stay for the memes."

And just to make sure the trolling was complete, he did one last thing; he changed his bio title on Twitter from the CEOs of Twitter and SpaceX to the fictitious "Former CEO of Dogecoin."

It was obviously one big joke, but as Freud might say, "Every joke is a truth wrapped in a smile," and Musk appeared to be expressing genuine interest in crypto and Bitcoin that night. The real truth was yet to reveal itself, but either way his tweets were sending crypto assets of all sizes on wild rides.

In January 2021, there were few hotter stocks than Tesla, and no bigger personality in the world than Musk. On January 8 of that year, a late-day surge sent Tesla shares up 5%, which moved Musk atop the world's ranking of richest people, with a staggering net worth of $188.5 billion. He just narrowly edged out Amazon founder Jeff Bezos.

Musk took a second to reflect on the moment by doing what he often does. He took to Twitter and posted, "How Strange." And later followed up with "Well, back to work."

Perhaps because of his ubiquitous presence on Twitter, Musk seemed to be everywhere, weighing in on every topic, from COVID mandates to other hot social topics. Occasionally he'd tweet about a SpaceX or Tesla business milestone. Other times, he'd tweet out inappropriate memes, usually with a cartoon image of a female in a suggestive pose. He'd taunt regulators and politicians alike and in doing so established himself as a global iconoclast, someone who was very much both part of the system and above it at the same time. This gave him unique credibility in the crypto community, which had always had a libertarian and antigovernment streak to it. After all, Bitcoin existed outside the system and was embraced by users who wanted a product that was not corrupted by central bank money printing or onerous regulations. They were reinventing the banking system by building a network that was revolutionizing centuries-old concepts about money and wealth. And they were doubted and ridiculed at every turn by some of the most well-respected people in the world: Warren Buffett, Jamie Dimon, Mark Cuban, Paul Krugman, Nouriel Roubini.

In Musk, crypto evangelist saw a kindred soul. Through SpaceX and Tesla in particular, he was redefining age-old industries while proving the naysayers wrong. By introducing mass-produced electric cars, Musk was upending the auto industry and taking it to the Big Three in Detroit. Critics howled. "Why would anyone want an electric car? Charging is too hard. The range is too low!" But Musk focused on the one thing that really matters: the consumer.

Teslas were cars in the sense that they had four wheels and doors. But that's where the similarities ended. They looked different. They drove different. They didn't have speedometers or clunky buttons. Instead, it was just one big iPad-looking device at the center of the car. It was faster and quieter than anything on the road. And because it was lighter, it was safer, too. It had the latest technology that could literally drive itself. It wasn't a car. It was a computer on wheels, and the faithful were sold. Investors took note and furiously bid up shares, much to the chagrin of critics, of which there were many. Tesla was always a heavily shorted stock, meaning investors were actually betting that shares would fall. They pointed to what they saw as poor fundamentals: few deliveries, loss per car, and lack of electric vehicle (EV) infrastructure. But obviously, they weren't looking at Tesla for what the company really was: a tech titan. Tesla was no more a car company than Netflix was a media stock, or Amazon a retailer.

In 2017, Tesla delivered about 103 000 cars, but it did something else that was considered at the time unthinkable: it passed GM to become America's most valuable carmaker. Why? Because while Tesla sold only 103 000 in 2017, its future looked brighter than that of any other automaker. Five years later, that number would grow to 1.8 million units. Tesla had cornered the market for electric cars, and every other automaker was now in a desperate chase to catch up.

Sound familiar? Tesla was the Bitcoin of automakers. It was transformative. It was the future of cars. And it didn't hurt that he was one of the founders of PayPal, an early electronic payments provider that was also founded by Peter Thiel, among others. Musk wasn't some billionaire who just happened to stumble upon Bitcoin. He had been working in the payment space before the payment space was a thing. He was the real deal – a visionary, an engineer, and a businessperson all wrapped up in one. And he had an anti-system anarchist streak that dovetailed nicely with the anti-establishment vibe of Bitcoin believers.

In short, Musk was already a hero to the crypto community. He was about to become a god.

On January 29, 2021, Musk, who at the time had 44 million followers, changed his Twitter bio from CEO of Tesla to just simply #Bitcoin. Crypto enthusiasts took note, sending Bitcoin prices 20% higher. Two days later, just to make sure his point was well taken, Musk returned to Twitter and said, "I do at this point think Bitcoin is a good thing, and I am a supporter of Bitcoin." Crypto investors were in a frenzy! Would he embrace the digital coin and add it to Tesla's balance sheet as Saylor suggested? Would the world's richest and most influential man, a person whose name sits beside the Mount Rushmore of inventors – da Vinci, Edison, Jobs – would this person come out publicly, put his money where his mouth was, and buy Bitcoin?

The answer came a week later, early in the morning on February 8. Tucked inside an 8-K filing that was posted with little fanfare, Tesla announced it had bought $1.5 billion worth of Bitcoin.

CNBC's Andrew Ross Sorkin broke the news and read aloud from the company's filing.

"Are you ready for this?" Sorkin asked viewers. "Tesla says it has 'updated our investment policy to provide us with more flexibility to further diversify and maximize returns on our cash that is not required to maintain adequate operating liquidity. As part of the policy. . .we may invest a portion of such cash in certain alternative reserve assets including digital assets, gold bullion, gold exchange-traded funds, and other assets as specified in the future. Thereafter, we invested an aggregate $1.5 billion in Bitcoin under this policy and may acquire and hold digital assets from time to time or long-term. Moreover, we expect to begin accepting Bitcoin as a form of payment for our products in the near future, subject to applicable laws and initially on a limited basis, which we may or may not liquidate upon receipt.'"

Twitter exploded and for the crypto faithful, it was bedlam. Almost immediately after reading the news, Bitcoin and shares of Tesla started to move higher, with Bitcoin reaching a then-record of $44 000 a coin. The implications for Bitcoin could not be overstated. One of the world's most valuable companies, founded and operated by one of the world's most influential businesspeople, had just openly embraced crypto in general and Bitcoin in particular. Would other tech giants follow suit? What if Apple decided to accept Bitcoin? What if Google did? The network would explode and drive coin prices even higher.

Katie Haun, a crypto expert at venture capitalist giant Andreessen Horowitz, took to Twitter to celebrate: "Big news for the crypto space this morning with @Tesla buying BTC for part of its treasury. What company or companies do you think will be next?"

Others were impressed by the size of Musk's bet, noting that it spoke to his conviction level. At the time, Tesla had about $20 billion in cash and short-term securities on its balance sheet. This move wasn't just some 1 to 2 % purchase, some empty signal to the crypto community. This was nearly 10% of available cash. That's putting your money where your mouth was. In a Securities Exchange Commission filing weeks earlier, then Tesla CFO Zachary Kirkhorn went on to update his title, adding the tongue-in-cheek moniker of "Master of Coin" beside "Chief Financial Officer."

It was the start of perhaps the most speculative year Wall Street had seen since 1999, the height of the dotcom bubble. "I know more people who have a SPAC than have COVID," quoted the *New York Times*, as a speculative mania grabbed the Street. Special-interest acquisition companies (SPACs) had been around for decades, but they exploded in popularity in the early days of 2021 as more and more companies raced to tap the public markets (unlike traditional initial public offerings (IPOs), SPACs faced fewer onerous listing requirements and allowed companies to go public faster). But it wasn't just SPACs – traditional IPOs were taking off, with some of the world's best-known names ready to exit the private markets.

Tech stocks exploded as investors and corporate America began to harness the power of technology. Cathie Wood's ARK Innovation fund, which invested in new and disruptive public companies, including Tesla, Zoom, and Teledoc, skyrocketed in popularity. Her daily changes to the fund would move stocks 3 to 4 %. By early 2021, most people were still working remotely from home. The COVID vaccine had just been rolled out, but very few had taken it yet, and most people were still working from home, spending ever more time on their computers and phones, and speculating on stocks and crypto. Many restaurants and bars were still closed or faced severe restrictions. Sporting events were either closed or played without spectators. Movies were not being released. There was really nothing to do other than watch cable television and Netflix, or trade stocks.

Millions of Americans were being reintroduced to stocks and crypto. David Portnoy of Barstool Sports fame started live streaming his trading session, going in and out of names like American Airlines – "We fly in this country!" he'd bellow to his millions of fans – like he was laying off a fourth-quarter bet. The online brokers, including Robinhood, E-Trade, and Charles Schwab, opened accounts at record paces. Coinbase, the wildly popular crypto exchange, was reporting record volume, which was timely as it was preparing to go public that year through a direct listing. Apple had just split its stock for the first time in seven years.

America was getting rich, and amid the speculative orgy of massive public spending, low rates, surging stocks, and idle time, Bitcoin was on fire. After breaking through $44 000, it headed right to a new record north of $64 000 on March 13. As a firm, it was hard not to be thrilled with what was happening. We pivoted in late 2020 and were now reaping the fruits of our prescient bet. Sure, we wished we had started acquiring coins when they were at $2000, but as we explained, we weren't comfortable with the initial infrastructure when we started looking at the space some years back. And while $64 000 was way higher than we thought Bitcoin would be three months after launching our fund, it was still way shy of where we thought it could be, which was at least $500 000 per coin.

As Brett Messing was often fond of pointing out, investors in the space are better off tracking the news rather than the price. "Whatever price you paid for Bitcoin, it was likely 10 times higher than when you first encountered it," said Messing. "And that's a hard thing to do. The people who bought it at $600 were likely introduced to it at $60. The people who bought at $6,000 were likely introduced to it at $600."

So how did it feel? It felt great. After initial trepidation from some clients (mainly our distributors), we were getting credit for leaning into progress and the future. We certainly weren't the first to embrace crypto and Bitcoin, but we were by no means the last, and we were well ahead of the industry.

But as the man says, no tree grows to the sky. With stocks doing nothing but going up and Bitcoin now above $60 000 – in just a couple of months, the price had ludicrously tripled – some sort of pullback seemed all but inevitable. And I knew that it would probably be a big one. What I didn't anticipate was what would cause it: *Saturday Night Live.*

On April 25, 2021, the producers at *Saturday Night Live* announced that Musk would host the show on May 8, alongside Miley Cyrus. Shortly after, Musk took to, what else, Twitter and tweeted, "Am hosting SNL on May 8th. Let's find out just how live Saturday Night Live really is."

The reaction was not kind. Some called for Lorne Michaels, the show's longtime producer, to be fired. Bowen Yang, one of the few young breakout stars, posted a sad emoji face on his Instagram account. Aidy Bryant, another star, posted a screenshot of a tweet by Bernie Sanders that read: "The 50 wealthiest people in America today own more wealth than the bottom half of our people. Let me repeat that because it is almost too absurd to believe: the 50 wealthiest people in this country own more wealth than some 165 MILLION Americans. That is a moral obscenity."

Musk's staggering wealth, coupled with his pointed tweets questioning COVID policy, had turned him from a beloved figure on the left to a more controversial one. I personally feel Musk is a genius whose contributions to humanity aren't fully yet understood. But during the raw emotional period of 2020, he had become a bit of a lightning rod. Either way, the announcement caught the attention of the world, and of crypto watchers in particular.

Following the announcement, prices for several crypto coins surged. Bitcoin jumped by more than 10% as investors wondered what the always unpredictable Musk might say. Would he make another Tesla announcement? Would he endorse Bitcoin or Dogecoin or perhaps some other cryptocurrency? Because so many of them trade continuously, 24 hours a day, seven days a week, people could trade these coins up to and even during the appearance.

The show was rather unremarkable. The jokes were meh. The most notable line came when Musk revealed he has Asperger's, but otherwise the whole thing felt like a bit of a letdown, an overhyped spectacle that lost its luster 10 minutes into the broadcast. But then something big happened.

As part of the Weekend Update segment, Musk played financial expert Lloyd Ostertag, who was reputedly going to explain what Bitcoin and crypto assets were. Musk appeared in a bowtie, looking very professorial. The host of the segment, Michael Che, asked him, "So what are cryptocurrencies?"

Musk gave a standard answer about blockchain technologies and named a few, including Bitcoin, Ethereum, and, of course, Dogecoin.

Che followed with, "What is Dogecoin?"

Musk gave another stock answer. "It was created in 2013 and has a circulating supply of 117 billion coins. It's the future of currency."

The skit proceeded along those lines for another couple minutes, with the hosts continually asking, "What is Dogecoin?"

Finally, Che asked, "So it's a hustle?"

"Yeah, it's a hustle," Musk sheepishly offered, much to the delight of the crowd.

But investors weren't laughing, and the price of Bitcoin, Doge, and cryptos soon tumbled. Some of it may have been a "buy the rumor, sell the news" event. Crypto had run up in advance of the appearance. But the manner in which he dismissed Doge, and by extension the whole space, as a "hustle" gave nervous Bitcoin investors reason to take some profits. Maybe he wasn't the true Bitcoin believer after all. Maybe like Dogecoin, his whole involvement was a joke. It was never easy to tell what Musk's real motives were.

But Musk wasn't finished, and any doubt about his crypto commitment was settled just four days later, when he went on Twitter and said Tesla would not accept Bitcoin due to its impact on fossil fuels, a total reversal from just a couple months earlier.

"Tesla has suspended vehicle purchases using Bitcoin. We are concerned about rapidly increasing use of fossil fuels for Bitcoin mining and transactions, especially coal, which has the worst emissions of any fuel," Musk wrote. "Cryptocurrency is a good idea on many levels and we believe it has a promising future, but this cannot come at a great cost to the environment."

Bitcoin prices, which had been falling in the wake of the Doge "hustle" comment, were now in freefall. And they wouldn't stop falling until at least another month, when they finally bottomed out around $29 000, a nearly 50% decline. To many, Musk's actions smacked off one big joke. Musk touts Bitcoin. Prices surge. Then he mocks it, and the whole thing collapses. It briefly validated the worst of the critics, who falsely claimed the whole thing was bullshit.

Still, even Muck couldn't kill the speculative mania that was 2021, and Bitcoin would have one more big push to it, reaching a high of nearly $70 000 in November 2021.

Chapter Ten

A Little Bit of Salt

IN SEPTEMBER 2021, A SkyBridge tradition resumed after a yearlong hiatus caused by the pandemic: the SALT Conference. Every May since 2009, we had held our annual SkyBridge Alternative Conference (SALT) in Las Vegas.

Our first one was held in Vegas during the depths of the financial crisis. In our view, it was a way to differentiate ourselves from other asset managers, and it also sent a strong statement to the Street. We weren't just going to survive the Great Financial Crisis; we were going to come out the other side stronger.

But this wasn't going to be your average financial conference that people hate going to. It would be exciting and fun – intellectually stimulating but wildly entertaining at the same time. It would be the best party you could ever hope to attend, and you'd make fantastic industry contacts and grow your business. You didn't have to come. You wanted to come.

The plan was simple: get the biggest names in business, politics, and pop culture and put them together for a series of panels that covered everything from the S&P 500 to Middle East tensions to topics from the world of entertainment and sports. Magic Johnson spoke. Dan Loeb was there. David Tepper held a panel. Former President George W. Bush spoke. Think Davos without the cold weather and mounds of pretentiousness. Thought leadership and investing were brought together in Vegas. And for good measure, at the end of the evening, Train would perform. If I've learned anything from my time on Wall Street, it's that white guys love Train. We were in a class of our own.

Since that first SALT conference in 2009, it had been enormously additive to our business and to our customers' businesses as well. And then in 2020 COVID hit. Like many others on Wall Street, our funds were crushed by March. We did not anticipate COVID to be as far-reaching and devastating as it was. We thought it would be something along the line of other respiratory infections that had slowed regions economically but never shut down life. Our fund was hammered, and we had the worst two-week losses in our firm's history. But the financial toll was dwarfed by the personal devastation we witnessed first-hand in New York. Hospitals were overrun. The city was brought to its knees. We closed down our office. Everyone went to work remotely. There would be no SALT conference that year. Vegas, like everywhere else in the world, was still closed in May 2020. But the market recovered. We survived. Our loyal customers stayed with us and recouped their losses. Our late-year pivot into Bitcoin turned out to be a lifesaver, and by 2021 we were thriving again as a firm.

The new normal was nothing like the old, but in 2021, the world and the United States was trying to get back to some semblance of normality. Vaccines were making their way through the population. People were starting to resume in-person activities like indoor dining and sporting events, albeit masked in many cases. At SkyBridge, we took the highest precautions. You had to be vaxxed and tested to come into the office. But we, too, wanted to get back to some of our old traditions.

SALT has always been a defining event for our company, and now with the pivot into Bitcoin, it stands to be an even greater opportunity for us. Crypto was disrupting the financial services industry in the same way the Internet did 20 years before, and every market participant – from asset managers to chief technology officers to bankers – wanted to know how this fast-growing technology would impact their business. Bitcoin was also a hot topic for political leaders, too, as they sought to define a regulatory structure for this asset class.

We had held panels on crypto as part of past SALT conferences. Mike Novogratz was a regular. The Winklevoss twins spoke at another. But this SALT would be different. We would take the opportunity to introduce early Bitcoin adopters, like Wences Casares and Peter Briger, to traditional finance professionals who may be on the fence about crypto. And we wouldn't just talk Bitcoin. We'd get into the nuts and bolts of the business. Blockchain infrastructure. Altcoins. Custody solutions. All the arcane topics that might come up at a traditional investing conference, but with a crypto focus. We were already one of the more high-profile crypto asset managers. We should market ourselves as such and stick to the plan that worked so well for us in the past: get the smartest people in the room and talk about investing, politics, culture, and now Bitcoin!

"Let's reach out to the Bellagio and see if they can take us," I told my team.

We had signed a contract at the Bellagio for May 2020, but that was rendered moot as the hotel was closed. In 2021, May seemed too soon, so we looked for something later in the year, around September. We began lining up our list of luminaries and investors. Recently elected Mayor Adams, who announced that New York City would accept Bitcoin, was in. Ray Dalio committed. So did Novogratz and Loeb. Cathie Wood and Steve Cohen would join, as would Paris Hilton and Joe Torre (hey, gotta keep it fun) among others. But we added a number of voices from the world of crypto too, including Dan Morehead from Pantera; Jeremy Allaire of Circle; Asiff Hirji, the former head of Coinbase; and Sam Bankman-Fried (more on that later) among others. It was going to be our most important SALT conference since our first one.

But there was a problem.

"Our sponsors don't want to go to Vegas," my partner John Darsey told me over Zoom. "They're too concerned about travel."

Late 2021 was still a tenuous time in terms of public health and safety. Many people simply did not feel comfortable traveling to, and staying in, uncontrolled venues.

"What would they want to do?" I asked John.

"Well, they're willing to do an event in New York. That's what they are willing to do."

"Looks like we're doing New York!" I said.

In hindsight, New York made perfect sense. The city was ground zero for COVID, and it was just coming back to life. Much like Bitcoin itself, you could try to crush the Big Apple, but you could never kill it. It always comes back.

It's resilient, durable, and always strong. Our conference would be a statement to the world: New York was back and so, too, was SkyBridge. Of course, we took extra measures to make sure we were operating under the safest conditions. Attendees had to show proof of vaccination. At the end of the event, the Chainsmokers performed.

The feedback was overwhelming, but what struck me most was the response from traditional equity asset managers. The conference brought together this incredible combination of early adopters and traditional asset managers, sharing panels and exchanging ideas about the future of finance. I was a little unsure how many of them would respond to the inclusion of so much crypto-related content. It was as much a crypto conference as it was a traditional investing one, but by late 2021, the lines between the two worlds were beginning to merge. But pretty much every client came up to us and said how much they loved it and how informative they thought the whole experience was. If you were a Bitcoin OG, SkyBridge was late to the game. If you were a traditional asset manager, we were early. We somehow managed to get credit from both groups – certainly no easy feat. It didn't hurt that Bitcoin was surging and just two months away from making all-time highs.

Years later, Bitcoin is as much a part of the SALT conference as anything else. We've even introduced a Wyoming Blockchain Symposium, an invitation-only event that will bring together the top investors, policymakers, and entrepreneurs from the digital asset space, just before the Fed hosts its Jackson Hole Symposium. Talk about counterprogramming! We'll be at the Four Seasons hosting coin founders. That is way more interesting than the central bankers.

In the end, SALT 2021 was more than just a conference. It was a statement to the world on demonstrating financial services leadership, for both New York and the world. It was about demonstrating our commitment to this new and emerging technology that was transforming the financial landscape. It was a statement about resilience in all its forms.

We would need it. The next year was going to be very tough.

Chapter Eleven

The Start of the
Crypto Winter

SALT NY WAS AN unqualified triumph. But around that time, the party ended for all risk assets. The bell never rings at the top, and there was no clear-cut catalyst for the decline in overall markets. But after surging 35% in 2019, 43% in 2020 (few called that run in March 2020), and 21% in 2021, the Nasdaq Composite needed a breather. And it got one in a big way.

For much of 2020 and 2021, low rates and unprecedented fiscal and monetary stimulus propped up the economy and lifted all asset prices. But the real economy was still largely closed. People weren't traveling as much. Restaurants were largely shuttered. Most people were working from home. That all started to change in 2022, and the physical economy reopened with a bang. Long-dormant supply chains became ensnared and supply constraints ensured, leading to a generational surge in interest rates and a return to 1970s-style inflation. As rates rose, investors began to reprice tech and high-growth stocks in particular. If an asset was speculative, it was sold. Special-interest acquisition companies (SPACs) cratered, and sure enough, Bitcoin was sold hard.

Clients began to call. And we would remind them of Brett Messing's favorite saying: "Pay attention to the news, not the price action."

It was easier said than done. But an interesting pattern started to emerge in 2022: tech and Bitcoin become increasingly correlated. The Nasdaq 100, which is the best broad measure of technology stocks, started to trade with Bitcoin. Growth and the expectation of future cash flows are the main drivers for that index, and as a result, it's much more sensitive to rising rates as investors call into question the future value of those earnings. If you believe Bitcoin is a growth asset and that its value will be determined by how fast its network grows, then logic would follow that it, too, would be subject to the same forces that drive traditional risk assets like growth stocks.

But Bitcoin faced bigger problems that Fall. On November 2, 2022, Coindesk, a crypto industry publication, reported that FTX, one of the world's largest crypto exchanges, was commingling funds between its own internal hedge fund and those of its customers. The report spooked its clients and other crypto market participants. A bank run soon ensued, and on November 11, FTX filed for Chapter 11 bankruptcy. Assets were frozen. It was the quickest collapse of a financial firm since Enron's some 20 years earlier. The event set off a series of convulsive shocks through the financial markets and confirmed the worst suspicions of all crypto haters. It was Mt. Gox all over again, and maybe even worse. It amplified the voices who had long called crypto a scam and a Ponzi. FTX's place in the financial universe cannot be overstated. Its investors included a who's who in the world of venture capital, including Sequoia Capital, Thoma Bravo, Tiger Global, and Temasek among others, not to mention slew of celebrities. SkyBridge Capital was also an investor. It was valued at more than $35 billion, more than the Nasdaq. FTX's founder, Sam Bankman-Fried, with his trademarked wild hair and baggy shorts, was as well-known as any of the celebrities or athletes who endorsed his product. As a brand, it was as well-known as Goldman Sachs.

On November 3, nearly one year to the day when that Coindesk article was released, Bankman-Fried was convicted of fraud for stealing $10 billion from customers. On March 28, he was sentenced to 25 years in prison.

I have said publicly everything I can about my relationship with Bankman-Fried and his family, and this book is not the place to rehash all that. A jury of his peers found him guilty, and now he is paying the price, as he should.

But something else notable happened weeks after FTX filed for bankruptcy: Bitcoin bottomed. On November 21, Bitcoin hit a low of around $15 745, and never looked back. I could not disagree more with Warren Buffett about his views on Bitcoin, but he is 100% correct when he says, "Be fearful when others are greedy. Be greedy when others are fearful."

I believe that day in November marked a generational low for Bitcoin, in much the same way 666 marked the bottom for the S&P 500 on March 3, 2009. It's always darkest before dawn, and few days have been darker for me than those fateful ones. But perversely, it might have been one of the best things that could've happened to Bitcoin and crypto. It showed that Bitcoin is bigger than its biggest exchange. It showed that Bitcoin is bigger than its biggest personalities, and in doing so, it showed the same resilient qualities that helped it go from $0.01 to $70 000. It was proof of the Lindy Effect in real life. First put forth by Albert Goldman in an article in the *New Republic*, the Lindy Effect posited that a comedian's longevity was in direct relation to how often he appeared on television. Later, Nassim Nicholas Taleb of

Black Swan fame and, ironically, a noted Bitcoin hater, would tweak that idea into a theory about survivability. According to Taleb, for "the nonperishable, every additional day may imply a longer life expectancy. The robustness of an item is proportional to its life." In other words, what doesn't kill you makes you stronger, and if Bitcoin has survived this long, chances are it's likely to exist in the future, too.

Bitcoin didn't need Bankman-Fried after all. It didn't need FTX. And those who sold did so in fear. The technology behind Bitcoin hadn't changed. If anything, it was getting better. The network was growing. The exchanges and the broker dealers may have facilitated access to Bitcoin, but they didn't change what Bitcoin was: the world's first and only truly decentralized store of value.

Bitcoin was bigger than its baddest of bad actors. It was here to stay.

When the smoke cleared at the end of 2022, Bitcoin lost 64% of value, its second worst annual performance. Meanwhile, the Nasdaq Composite lost 33%, registering its worst annual performance since the Great Financial Crisis. And the industry suffered major reputational damage. But Bitcoin had been through similar challenges before, and the smart money knew better than to panic.

In fact, rather than run from Bitcoin and crypto, a new and crucial chapter was about to begin, and Wall Street would come calling in a way it never had before.

Chapter Twelve

Wall Street Comes Calling

———— ∾ ————

"I KEEP GETTING ASKED about Bitcoin," John Normand remarked on JP Morgan's morning call. It was 2014, and Normand was sitting atop his newly minted perch as head of FX & Commodities International Rates Research. The Euro and Aussie Dollar were crashing, but all of Normand's clients, particularly those out of Australia, wanted to know about this new Internet money called Bitcoin.

"It's the darndest thing," Normand added.

Tom Lee looked up from his desk. As JP Morgan's equity strategist, it was Lee's job to synthesize mountains of data – from interest rates around the world to the myriad of inputs spit out each day by the stock market – and recommend one of two things for his clients based on all that information: buy or sell. But many of those same clients had begun asking questions about Internet money. These clients weren't mom-and-pop retail investors. They weren't registered investment advisors or your typical financial advisors. They were institutional clients. Hedge funds. Endowments. The behemoths. And they all seemed to be fascinated with a new currency that collectively was worth about $50 billion.

It got Lee very curious. At the time, Bitcoin was so new that it was almost impossible for an institutional investor to express an investment thesis on the digital currency. Still, it remained the subject of much fascination among some of JP Morgan's global macro clients and the subject of much speculation on JP Morgan's trading desks. Around this time, Bitcoin was trading between $400 and $1000, but it wasn't the volatility that caught the group's attention. It was the idea of a truly decentralized currency – that is to say, one that wasn't created by a central bank – that captivated the group.

The interest never materialized into anything concrete. JP Morgan did not get involved in the space until years later, but the bug had been planted in Lee's mind. When he left the firm to start his own in the fall of 2014, he continued to publish widely read and thoughtful (and crazily accurate) pieces about the stock market, but his real fascination was with this new asset class: Bitcoin.

As a former technology analyst, Lee was always looking for a long-term growth story that could last 5–10 years, and this new mysterious asset class fit the bill. He dove into everything he could find about the subject, reading everything and talking to everyone he could about how the blockchain worked and what drove Bitcoin prices. He soon started to notice a pattern: the price of Bitcoin, in the longer term at least, was driven mostly by the number of wallets and how active those wallets were. Bitcoin, it would seem, wasn't just some speculative asset whose price was derived from nothing. It was based on a principle of long-standing value – Metcalfe's law again!

So in July 2017, Lee did something very bold: he became the first credible Wall Street strategist to publish a research note on Bitcoin. Now, today that seems commonplace. Every major Wall Street firm has some crypto business, and equity strategists are routinely looking toward Bitcoin and crypto to glean the stock market's next move. But at the time, in summer of 2017, major Wall Street strategists just weren't publishing on the topic.

To make matters even more interesting, the title of the piece raised eyebrows up and down the Street: "By 2022, Bitcoin could be worth $12,000 to $55,000 per unit" read the report.

At the time, Bitcoin was trading around $2600 and had just run up 173% that year, so the call seemed almost foolishly optimistic, and financial media was quick to point out that Lee had been incorrectly bearish on equities (though a late summer swoon would soon prove his bearish calls accurate).

Clients howled. Some fired his firm right on the spot. One prominent hedge fund manager, whose pedigree included working for a veritable Mount Rushmore of investment managers, fired off a frosty email.

"I cannot believe you are writing this garbage, and I no longer want to be a client."

"You're losing credibility," howled another very famous octogenarian over the phone, spit likely forming on the edges of his mouth. "No one cares about this stuff!!"

While the stodgy old men were aghast, another group of investors were thrilled. Family offices lapped it up. Retail investors who caught his appearances on CNBC couldn't stop retweeting his clips. There was a virality to the space that bordered on obsession. It was more than just an investment. It was a passion that ran deeper than simply numbers.

"It was really eye-opening," said Lee. "I was shocked at how many investors, both traditional retail and professional as well, owned Bitcoin."

His research was filling a void on Wall Street, and perhaps to the chagrin of the establishment but much to the delight of retail, Lee's call turned out to be maybe one of the most precinct ever made.

Lee saw what few others on the Street did at the time: Bitcoin would soon become a digital substitute for gold.

At the time, the total value of the gold market stood at around $7.5 trillion, making it the third-largest asset class behind fixed income and equities. Unlike others, Lee viewed Bitcoin more as a store of value as opposed to a form of payment. According to his work, Bitcoin could eventually represent 5% of the total gold's total market, giving it a unit price of $55 000, more than 20 times what Bitcoin was trading for in July 2017.

But as his note pointed out, the supply of mined Bitcoins was rapidly falling. In fact, in July 2017, the number of newly mined Bitcoins had actually fallen by half from the previous year, from 1.2 million to around 700 000 coins. Greater power needs to mine Bitcoin, combined with shrinking block rewards, would continue to slow the growing supply of future coins. Either way, the total number of Bitcoins that can ever be mined is capped at 21 million. In contrast, despite that 98% of all gold mined was still in existence, gold supply was actually increasing at 1.5%. Plus, gold is an extraterrestrial material, meaning there's a plentiful supply of gold zooming around the universe in the form of comets and asteroids. So, whereas Bitcoin's scarcity is fixed, gold's is really just a function of how aggressive miners want to dig.

But what Lee was really identifying was a generational difference in investor preferences.

"Older investors like gold," Lee would later say. "Gold had its biggest price appreciation when the dollar went off the gold standard. And so that generation that adopted gold [was] really, essentially, children of the Great Depression. They witnessed first-hand financial calamities. So, if you were 50 years old in the '70s, you were a child of the Depression. But beyond jewelry, gold isn't nearly as popular with young people. Young people view Bitcoin as sounder money than gold."

Lee is 100% correct. Gold was my parents' hedge against inflation. It surged when Nixon took the United States off the gold standard and inflation surged in the 1970s and '80s. But since then, the better hedge against inflation was the stock market. Gold is old Wall Street and, for all intents and purposes, completely impractical. Are you really going to go to Walmart and shave off a portion of your gold bar? It's an ineffective medium to transact with. You can carry and transport a million dollars' worth of Bitcoin in the palm of your hand and send it around the world instantly. Try sending a million dollars' worth of gold bars anywhere. Gold's industrial uses, which supposedly imbue it with some intrinsic value, are at best limited. Lastly, gold can be damaged or tainted.

"It's sort of an irrational trade if you really think about it," said Lee.

But there's an even bigger problem. Older libertarians may flock to gold as a hedge against the end of the world, against societal collapse, and to some extent, many Bitcoin investors buy the cryptocurrency for the same reasons. What I've learned over time is that the world never ends. The sun always rises and sets. But in the exceedingly rare chance that society does collapse, would you rather be walking around with a bag of gold bars or with a completely traceable store of value on your phone? For a generation that grew up using computers, the answer is easy.

Isn't that incredible? A material that has been coveted for 6000 years by societies all over the world is less practical and likely to be less valuable than a virtual substance that has existed for only 15 years. It's a mind-blowing concept if you think about it.

For those keeping score at home, Bitcoin hit $55 000 in early 2021, one year ahead of Lee's original target. The customers who dumped him are probably still screaming at him. The future is not for the faint of heart.

But it was a precursor of what was to come. Wall Street was taking notice, and although Bitcoin existed and, to some extent, derived its value by functioning outside the traditional financial systems, it was only a matter of time before it would begin to join it.

Chapter Thirteen

From Butter
to Bitcoin

"TERRY, WHAT ARE YOU going to do about Bitcoin?" asked John Willian, the Goldman Sachs lifer who was running the firm's vaunted fixed income department. He was joined by Goldman's president, Gary Cohn, and the Terry he was talking to was the one and only Terry Duffy, the chief executive officer (CEO) of the Chicago Mercantile Exchange (CME), the world's largest publicly traded exchange. The CME has always been at the forefront of the financial services industry, starting way back when it was the Chicago Butter and Egg Board in 1898. Farmers would bring their crops to Chicago to sell it to distributors, who would then turn around and ship it all over the world. The futures market provided a more efficient way to manage costs. The farmer would get cash in exchange for delivering a set amount of wheat, eggs, or another commodity at a future date (leading to the name "futures"). In other words, the futures market provided a tool to mitigate and manage risks for both the buyer and the seller.

Fast-forward almost 200 years, and the CME is still offering the same service, except now the product offering is much bigger. You can buy futures on pretty much anything: oil, gold, S&P 500, Nasdaq 100, interest rates, the dollar. If there is a financial product, chances are there's a futures product associated with it, and chances are it trades on the CME, which is still based in Chicago and, since 2002, has been run by one Terry Duffy. Although he sits atop the very highest perch in corporate America, he's never forgotten his middle-class roots from the Southwest Side of Chicago, a neighborhood of cops and firefighters. During summers in college, he would work at Chuck's Bar, in Lake Geneva, Wisconsin, where he made drinks for visiting traders. In 1980, one of them offered him a job as a runner on the floor. There was no looking back. And in a 40-year career, he saw every type of market and product traded. Except this.

"Which coin?" he replied.

"*Bit*coin, Terry," Willian said slowly, emphasizing the first syllable. "It's all everyone's talking about."

Duffy looked over to Gary Cohn, who was leaning back against his desk with a big grin face, in hopes that he would let him in on the joke.

"I have no idea what the hell you are talking about, man. I never heard of a *Bit*coin," said Duffy, who also emphasized the first syllable.

The room broke out into laughter.

"All I know is clients keep talking about it," Cohn said to more laughter. "It's this crazy virtual currency. They say it could change the world," Cohn added before flashing his trademark grin.

It was 2013, and Duffy was at Goldman headquarters in lower Manhattan on a routine visit to the firm to meet with clients. He had known Willian for years and always enjoyed talking with Cohn when he was in town. They discussed some other business matters and then Duffy was off. But later that night he couldn't stop thinking about the day and his conversation with Willian and Cohn about this new digital currency. It struck him as odd that two of the most senior members of Goldman Sachs were so captivated by this new digital currency, this *Bit*coin.

He began doing some online research to learn more about it and about the broader history of digital currencies, none of which ever really panned out. Still, as a former trader and floor broker, the chart caught his eye. This virtual currency, this "Bitcoin," had gone in one direction since it started trading: up. It had gone from $1 in 2011 to $100 in 2013. He really didn't know what to make of it beyond the fact that it seemed a great vehicle for speculation. But the trader in him suspected there was more there.

That suspicion was confirmed a couple weeks later at his annual Global Financial Leadership Conference, which the CME hosts every year. Industry watchers bill it the Davos of Derivatives, where CME brings together thought leaders in business, politics, and culture. But this year it was different. All anyone could talk about was this incredible surge in Bitcoin. Over the span of four days, Bitcoin went from just over $200 to nearly $1000. In one day alone it doubled. In some ways, it was like a precursor to GameStop or AMC during the "meme stock" craze. But this was 2013, and Duffy, who had seen pretty much everything, had never seen a move like this.

He sought out some attendees that he knew had played around with the digital currency.

"What is this stuff?" Duffy asked one of them. "It was 10 bucks just a couple months ago. It's 1000 bucks!"

Now Bitcoin had Duffy's attention.

He really couldn't tell what the use case for this new thing was. It was obviously too volatile to be a very useful payment system. But it sure was capturing a lot of people's attention, and some of those people were his customers.

Whenever Duffy wanted to know about a new technology or product in trading, he'd call one of his oldest acquaintances from the floor, Billy DiSomma. DiSomma started Jump Trading, an early pioneer in high-frequency trading that became a dominant wholesaler. DiSomma knew about two things better than just about anyone: trading and technology.

"It's the future," DiSomma told Duffy over the phone. DiSomma had been one of the earliest Bitcoin investors that Duffy knew. He had been trading and learning about it for years. And in Bitcoin, DiSomma saw the future. "Maybe market structure stays the same for the next hundred years," he said. "But I tend to doubt it. And I suspect this stuff will be at the center of whatever it is."

And there it was, straight from one of Duffy's most trusted brains. Whatever Bitcoin turns or doesn't turn out to be, it would be at the center of innovation, and if history has shown anything, it's that turning your back on the future, particularly esoteric and scary ones, is a recipe for ruin.

Duffy looked out his office window and saw old Sears Tower, the former headquarters to Sears, Roebuck & Co. At one point, Sears was the world's largest retailer, with nearly 350000 employees. Sears was the Amazon of its day. The company began by selling a single product (wristwatches) via mail catalog, which was sort of like the Internet of its time. Eventually, it moved into other categories, allowing people access to previously unavailable products. Sears continued to grow and innovate, putting customer needs above anything else by offering them anything they could possibly want, either by catalog or in one of their many pristine locations. They even acquired Dean Whitter Reynolds in 1981 in an ill-fated effort to serve customers' financial needs. Rivals dismissively referred to it as "Stocks & Socks."

Sears eventually got so big that the company decided it needed a new corporate headquarters in downtown Chicago. When completed in 1973, the Sears Tower stood at 110 stories and at 1454 ft, making it the world's tallest building, a distinction held for 25 years. But like many dominant companies, Sears began to rest on its laurels, and soon enough, competition caught up – first Walmart, which passed it in market cap in 1991, and later Amazon, which ultimately killed it. In 2018, it filed for bankruptcy. Now its former headquarters stands as both a monument to innovation and a cautionary tale for companies that ignore it. In 2009, its revered tower was renamed the Willis Tower.

Was crypto the world's savior? Probably not, thought Duffy. But a lot of really smart people were fascinated by it, including himself. And he realized that if this new asset class had a more credible central marketplace, then more market participants could begin to use it.

Over the next couple months and years, that interest would grow, with more and more clients inquiring about Bitcoin. While heavily traded on crypto-native exchanges like Coinbase and others, Bitcoin had not found a home on an established traditional exchange. Customers, which included futures brokers and hedge funds, were increasingly looking for a way to express a view on Bitcoin in a more regulated, traditional financial arena, and the Chicago Board Options Exchange (CBOE) and CME were beginning to explore the possibility of adding this product. But to Duffy, offering a Bitcoin derivative was about more than just serving customers and staying ahead of the competition.

Whether it was gold or a payment system didn't really matter. Bitcoin represented financial progress and innovation, two principles that had guided the CME to success for more than a century. The Chicago Egg & Butter Board was running a healthy business in two of the most popular agricultural products of its time. There's no doubt the early founders could've ridden that well into retirement. But they didn't. They pushed into other markets, ones outside their traditional expertise. Now, trillions of dollars' worth of products trade every day on the CME.

Of course, entering this new market was not without risk. For every customer who wanted Bitcoin futures, there was an equally important one against it, and making the product widely available may force some brokers to offer a product they don't want for fear of losing out to a rival.

And then there were the haters.

"There's no way you can offer this product. Terry, this is crazy!" hollered one influential advisor. Reputationally, there was a lot at stake. If this product didn't work, it would be a major black eye for the CME. But Duffy felt the inexorable pull of progress. If you don't change, you'll be left out.

Duffy summoned his team to his office.

Brimming with excitement, he could hardly sit down.

"Today's the day!" he proclaimed. There was a brief pregnant pause before one of his lieutenants spoke up.

"The day for what?"

"Bitcoin. Call the CFTC and tell them we're gonna list this thing," Duffy said. "Look, I'm a big believer in timing. I've seen a lot of people make a lot of money when they're wrong. And I've seen a lot of people lose a lot of money when they're right. It's just timing. And I've looked at Bitcoin. The price doesn't matter to me. The timing does, and the timing is right now."

There were myriad technical challenges, and the exchange would go through extraordinary measures to make sure the product functioned properly and safely. Its margin requirement would be three times that of a standard S&P 500 contract. The Bitcoin futures contract had the highest margin requirement of any product the exchange had ever offered. If anything, this product was going to be safe. They worked extensively with their regulator, the

Commodity Futures Trading Commission (CFTC), to make sure everything was properly tested and retested. The only really effective way to mainstream a new financial product was to work closely with regulators to create a solid and dependable regulatory framework. The CME was going to slow-walk this product out of the gate, taking extra pains to make sure their customers felt comfortable with it. After all, if they were going to offer it to their customers, they needed to feel good about it.

On December 17, 2017, Terry walked through the front doors of the CME on an uncharacteristically warm winter Sunday in Chicago. New product launches typically aren't big deals, but this one was different. The world would be watching, and everything needed to be perfect. After years of financial engineering and tremendously challenging work, involving customers, regulators, and financial engineers, the product was ready. At 5 p.m. Central time, the product launched, and a price was displayed. After initially opening at just over $20 000, the contract bounced up and down a bit as it trailed its financial alter ego, spot Bitcoin.

Bitcoin was officially inserted into the financial matrix. Now, traditional financial investors had a venue and a product to express their view on this new and fascinating asset class, and they could do so on one of the world's oldest and most respected exchanges. From his office, Duffy stared at the quotes on his screen and one word kept coming to mind: progress. This exchange had gone from selling eggs to wheat to currency indexes to stock and bond indexes to something that didn't exist at all in physical form: cryptocurrencies. To this day Bitcoin remains on Duffy's watchlist.

He checks it multiple times a day.

Chapter Fourteen

Mr. Wonderful Has a Change of Heart

A soft breeze gently blew in from the vast expanse off Lake Geneva. Snow-covered Alps sparkled in the distance. The late autumn sun glistened off the cobalt-blue waters. It was heaven on Earth.

Kevin O'Leary picked up a glass of Le Montrachet Grand Cru, held it briefly to his nose, and took in a nice hearty sip. Wasn't as good as his own O'Leary Fine Wine Chardonnay, but it was as close to crisp perfection as one could hope for.

Nothing could ruin this moment.

"So Kevin," asked the gentleman sitting across from him in the thickest of German accents. "What do you think of Bitcoin?"

Except that.

The gorgeous colors of the mountains faded. The slight sounds of traffic off the always-bustling Grand Rue were suddenly audible. The smile that millions of *Shark Tank* fans had grown to love slowly morphed into a scoff of disbelief. The moment was ruined.

"What are you talking about?" O'Leary shot back.

"A lot of my clients are asking about it," his lunch companion asked. "They think it's a great asset class."

"Asset class?" O'Leary laughed out loud. "It's some guys writing code online. It's a video game!"

It was late 2015, and O'Leary was having lunch off Lake Geneva with one of his Swiss hedge fund clients. Lunch on Lake Geneva is always a grand affair, with an appetizer, main course, and a fine wine, usually at one of the many five-star hotels that line Montreux. As chairman of O'Shares, a leading exchange-traded fund (ETF) provider, O'Leary would routinely travel the world to meet with his investors, who were always on the hunt for exciting new technology opportunities. O'Leary could talk for hours about the wonders of Facebook (now Meta) or Amazon. He was a believer in new and disruptive technologies and would invest either directly in them or through his ETFs.

He is also an avid Rolex collector, so he understood how stores of value worked. But for whatever reason at that time, he was unable to put those two knowledge sets together and see that Bitcoin combined them both.

Instead, he chose to remain in the hater camp. "It's nothing but raw speculation. Where's the intrinsic value? They're gonna cut the number of new ones in half? That's a reason to buy it? It sounds like a scam. Stay away!" O'Leary implored his lunch companion, tapping into his considerable TV chops to muster all the dramatic enthusiasm he could.

His anti-crypto stance extended beyond that lunch. At frequent conferences and TV appearances, O'Leary rarely missed a chance to call Bitcoin "crypto crap." Part of his negative view was informed by regulators' antagonist stance against crypto – which he'd had firsthand experience with. You see, even though he wasn't a fan of buying or selling particular coins, he was a believer in the blockchain technology that underpinned all crypto coins and in the tokenization of physical assets. And in March 2018, he appeared on CNBC and said that he was working on a $400 million deal to allow a "very prestigious" New York hotel to sell ownership through an initial cryptocurrency offering (ICO), instead of a traditional initial public offering (IPO).

"Instead of a stock, a share, it's a coin," O'Leary said, while not revealing the name of the hotel. His ICO would adhere to standard US listing requirements. "The key is to make sure you go to the regulator and say, 'I want to work with you.'"

Apparently, the regulators did not get that memo. After O'Leary left the set, he hopped on a flight back to Miami. His phone had exploded with interest. The next day he was served by the Securities and Exchange Commission (SEC). They wanted to know about his involvement in the hotel.

"What's going on?" On the phone with his lawyer, he tried to make sense of the situation. "I haven't sold anything to anyone. We've been in contact with regulators."

"Gensler is trying to send a message to the marketplace," his attorney explained. "He hates crypto and wants to make an example of you. They hate this space."

It's unclear why SEC chair Gary Gensler has such an anti-crypto stance. Some have suspected it goes back to Senator Elizabeth Warren throwing her support behind him. She's been a long-time cynic of the financial system, and the unregulated aspects of crypto enrage her. Still, many crypto investors had high hopes for Gensler. He taught it at MIT, and as a former Goldman partner, many thought he'd openly embrace Bitcoin as a new asset class. But alas, he has not quite been the Prince of Crypto.

O'Leary cleared up the matter with the SEC in relatively short order. But the message was clear. Don't mess around with crypto or be prepared to have the agency up your ass.

So it was from an informed perspective that O'Leary told his German hedge fund client, "Don't touch this stuff. It's radioactive, and the regulators are dead set on crushing it." His stance didn't change much after that. Blockchain was a fascinating technology, certainly worth exploring and investing in, but the actual coins were a financial death wish, over-speculated on and sure to attract the wrong type of attention.

But then something happened. On February 12, 2021, the Ontario Securities Commission, Canada's most important securities regulator, cleared the launch of the first crypto exchange-traded fund. The Purpose Bitcoin ETF, sponsored by Purpose Investment Inc., was going to be the first ETF that directly invested in spot Bitcoin, rather than a futures product or other type of derivative. Up until that time, investors had only been able to purchase Bitcoin future contracts on the Chicago Mercantile Exchange (CME). Investors could also buy closed-end investment funds, but not an ETF that held "physically settled" Bitcoin, which was an ironic choice of words since Bitcoin is virtual by definition.

"That was a game-changer to me," O'Leary would later say.

In 2021, there were a number of US-based asset managers who were trying to introduce a spot Bitcoin ETF to the marketplace. But the SEC, particularly under Gensler, had adopted a scorched-Earth approach to anything crypto-related.

One week after the approval, North America's first spot Bitcoin ETF began trading. It exploded out of the gate, with investors trading more than $165 million in volume, far surpassing even the most optimistic estimates.

O'Leary's German clients were soon calling him up.

"What is going on, O'Leary? Did you see this?"

"I'll make some calls," O'Leary assured his client, as he promptly reached out to the various Canadian exchanges. The debut was a smashing success. There was little to no tracking error between the prices of spot Bitcoin and the Bitcoin ETF. It was seamless, like gold- or silver-tracking ETFs, despite that Bitcoin was much more volatile.

A new world had been opened up.

ETFs had been around for decades. The SPY and QQQ, which respectively track the S&P 500 and Nasdaq 100, have been longtime staples of the US markets. But in the past decade or so, their popularity has exploded, and ETFs have become more specialized, allowing investors to tailor or customize their exposure to a certain index or sector. ETFs provide access to oil, or a basket of soft commodities. They provide sector and industry access. They even allow you to own a whole index minus a particular sector. There are ETFs for banks, tech, airlines, and cybersecurity stocks. The S&P excluding oil. Europe, Japan, China. Chinese tech stocks. France. Mexico. Even the Magnificent 7, which is just Apple, Amazon, Alphabet, Microsoft, Nvidia, Tesla, and Meta, has its own ETF. I think you're starting to get the point. If you have an investment thesis, there's likely an ETF you can buy (or short) to express it. As of December 2023, the United States alone has 3000 different ETFs totaling over $8 trillion in assets. But until January 10, 2024, not one of them offered exposure to spot Bitcoin, despite Bitcoin being worth $ trillion.

O'Leary wondered how that could be. Institutions around the world were lining up to get exposure to this tiny Canadian ETF, which was approved by Canada's top regulator and listed on the Toronto Stock Exchange, but there was no alternative in the US, the most liquid and dynamic market in the world.

"Mooch, it doesn't make any sense," O'Leary would tell me over dinner in Dubai. "You can own Bitcoin as a direct proxy in an ETF wrapper in Canada but not in the United States? Everyone knows the [Ontario Securities Commission] and SEC are in constant communication. It's only a matter of time before the SEC follows suit and approves an US-based ETF."

O'Leary and I have known each other for years, through television, mutual friends, and the conference circuit. Although on different timetables, we've both embarked on similar crypto journeys, from initial skeptics to full-throated evangelists. My journey started from a different place: I was more indifferent and skeptical, while O'Leary was a full-on hater. But we arrived at more or less the same spot.

"I was wrong and the past is the past," O'Leary would later say. "This is the future. I guess the best way to look at this is, I believe what others do. Millions of people don't trust their governments to manage their fiduciary systems. There are people around the world in countries like Venezuela and Cuba and other places and they don't trust their government. They don't want to hold their paper. Bitcoin is their solution. And as the technology streamlines, it will only get bigger. Who am I to tell all these people they are wrong?"

O'Leary's point was simple: maybe there is wisdom in the crowds. It's clear that there is madness in crowds, and history has seen that over and over. But there is also wisdom in crowds. The herd is not always wrong, particularly when they don't start off as the herd. In the case of Bitcoin in 2019, the herd was certainly there, but it was a result of a movement that had been building for a decade and would continue to grow. The asset has gone from a penny a coin, exchanged between Hal Finney and Satoshi, to $70 000 a coin, exchanged among 300 million people.

What is more likely: those 300 million people, including some of the sharpest minds in finance, are all wrong and it's a tulip bubble, or that the people who have clung to outdated notions of finance are? My bet is with the former.

"I'm changing because the world changed, and it's my job to understand what's next, and Bitcoin is next," O'Leary said, before flashing his trademark smile.

Digital concepts are harder for people of my generation to accept. As a middle-class kid from Long Island who grew up with a passbook savings account, with a little book to record the debits and credits, the concept of money is different. It's physical. But for a generation of kids today who have grown up with computers and are more comfortable working in the virtual than the physical, digital assets aren't a stretch. In fact, they're logical. To them, digital assets are just an extension of the iPhone, or their virtual life. Physical coins are like VCRs, quaint to behold, maybe even cool to collect, but not practical.

O'Leary could already see the future.

"Trading cards. Collectables. Watches!" O'Leary exclaimed during that dinner. "All these things will need to be indexed like stocks, and the best technology to do that is the blockchain, and the best way to access any blockchain is through the native coins."

It was quite a change of heart, and I admired the openness of O'Leary's mind. He's a contemporary of mine, but he wasn't blinded by the past. More important, he was able to admit when he was wrong – one of the hardest things to do – and to reverse course, which is even harder! He would go on to take a much more aggressive position in Bitcoin, not only buying the underlying coin but also taking big stakes in various crypto exchanges, including ones in Canada and the Middle East.

The continued adoption of Bitcoin and the blockchain was a great tailwind for the industry. But to O'Leary and others, the real payout was the potential for a spot Bitcoin ETF.

"It is only a matter of time before the SEC approves an ETF," said O'Leary.

Chapter Fifteen

The ETFs Are Coming

On July 11, Michael Sonnenshein walked the storied floor of the New York Stock Exchange. His company's banners were everywhere. It was like a big initial public offering (IPO), and in many ways it was. He hadn't slept in 24 hours, but he wasn't tired. Less than 12 hours earlier, the Securities and Exchange Commission (SEC) granted approval for a spot Bitcoin exchange-traded fund (ETF). For Sonnenshein, an effervescent and eternally optimistic individual, the approval marked the end of a 10-year journey.

Grayscale was the asset management arm of Barry Silbert's Digital Currency Group, the crypto conglomerate that also owned Coindesk and Genesis Trading, among other businesses. Softbank was one of its investors, and the company at one point was valued at $10 billion. Sonnenshein had been chief executive officer (CEO) since 2021, but he had been the face of the firm since he was hired in 2013, when Silbert hired him to help raise assets for the firm, which at the time stood at $60 million. In those early days, investors were quick to dismiss them. Meetings were often canceled at the last minute or ended well before the allotted time. Still, Sonnenshein persevered, making regular appearances on financial media and appearing at countless conferences (including ours) in an effort to change investors' views on this emerging asset class.

Grayscale's major product was the Grayscale Bitcoin Investment Trust, which traded on the over-the-counter market under the ticker GBTC. It was the first major investment product to allow investors access to crypto without having to buy the underlying assets, or in the case of GBTC, Bitcoin. It was wildly popular with crypto-shy investors because it gave them exposure to Bitcoin without having to open an account on a crypto exchange and hold Bitcoin directly. The product also allowed investors to have exposure to Bitcoin in their individual retirement accounts (IRAs). Large-asset managers who wanted exposure to Bitcoin could look to GBTC as well. In a short time, it became one of the more popular ways for crypto-hesitant investors to gain access to the space. Its assets swelled to nearly $30 billion. ETFs owned it. Pension funds owned it. Endowments, foundations, and hedge funds all owned it. If you wanted to buy Bitcoin but didn't want to go through the hassle of owning cryptocurrencies directly, GBTC was your only real option. But it had an issue. It wasn't an ETF, it was a trust, and as such, was an imperfect vehicle for owning Bitcoin.

ETFs allow investors exposure to a particular asset class, index, or even investment strategy. They trade just like stocks on an exchange. But to make sure that the underlying asset is tracking the value of the ETF, or its net asset value (NAV), issuers engage in a process called *creation and redemption*. This prevents "slippage" and keeps the unit value of the ETF in line with the asset it is tracking. If, for example, a gold ETF started to trade at premium to gold, the issuer would work with its market makers and liquidity providers to create more shares to make sure the price of the ETF was in line with the asset it tracked. But because GBTC was not an ETF, it lacked the ability to engage in this process, and the result was price action more akin to a closed end mutual fund; at times it traded at a steep premium to NAV, at other times a discount. Bitcoin prices drove GBTC, but so too did extraneous market forces, and as a result, there were times where the price of GBTC was out of whack with Bitcoin.

Still, it was the most popular way to get exposure to the asset class through an equity-like investment.

Grayscale created the fund in 2013 hoping that one day it could transition into an ETF.

The SEC had other ideas.

In 2017, Cameron and Tyler Winklevoss lobbied the SEC to convert its Winklevoss Bitcoin Trust into an ETF. The SEC promptly rejected the Winklevoss' application, citing among other things the nature of Bitcoin itself and the exchanges on which it traded. The SEC felt crypto exchanges lacked the necessary controls to prevent market manipulation. A second application was rejected a year later.

Grayscale was smart. They played the long game. They had applied to convert GBTC from a private placement to an ETF, but after the Winklevoss' rejection, they withdrew their application. But then, quietly, starting in 2018, they began to engage the SEC in hopes of bringing GBTC further into the regulatory perimeter. They proposed the idea of making the fund an SEC-reporting entity. The SEC said no but came back later and agreed. In 2020, Grayscale officially became a SEC-reporting entity, which meant it had to file a number of standard reports, including 10-Qs, 10-Ks, and the like. The move was made to further assure crypto-shy investors about Grayscale's product and potentially open the product to a wider array of investors. It was also a good-faith measure on Grayscale's part to work with its regulator in a collaborative fashion.

In October 2021, after rejecting a number of spot Bitcoin ETFs, the SEC approved a Bitcoin futures ETF, which was sponsored by ProShares and listed on the New York Stock Exchange. It was a big step in the right direction toward a spot Bitcoin ETF. Investors could now purchase an equity-like product that traded on an exchange and had exposure to Bitcoin. But the product held Bitcoin futures, not actual Bitcoin. Investing in futures is not the same as investing in the underlying asset in the spot or cash market. The futures ETF tracked the cash-settled futures contract, not the price itself, and although they were very closely correlated, because of technical dynamics in the futures market, it wasn't quite the same thing. Think of it as Coke versus Diet Coke: they taste similar enough, but they're very different products for very different consumers.

The SEC approved the Bitcoin futures ETF because the Bitcoin futures market was overseen by the Commodity Futures Trading Commission (CFTC), and Bitcoin futures traded on the Chicago Mercantile Exchange (CME), a highly regulated exchange. And this tiny but crucial distinction would help pave the way for GBTC to become an ETF. It probably didn't hurt that the SEC commissioner, Gary Gensler, had also served as the CFTC chair, so there was likely some familiarity there, too.

Following the approval of the Bitcoin futures ETF, Grayscale resubmitted its plans to the SEC to become an ETF – and was rejected again. But this time, Grayscale wouldn't quietly shrink back to its corner. Grayscale management had anticipated a number of scenarios, including a rejection, and immediately sued the agency in June 2022, turning their logic against them. The SEC had long contended that Bitcoin exchanges lacked the proper surveillance to prevent market manipulation, but in contrast, the agency said the Bitcoin futures market was surveillable because it was overseen by the CFTC. The problem with that logic was that the two markets were in fact 99% correlated, and in Grayscale's view, if the surveillance arrangements for the Bitcoin futures ETF were satisfactory, then that should be good enough for spot Bitcoin ETFs as well, since both ultimately rely on the price of Bitcoin.

On August 29, 2023, the appellate court ruled 3-0 in favor of Grayscale. In the court's view, the proposed Bitcoin ETF was materially similar to the existing Bitcoin futures ETFs, and since the two assets were so closely correlated, the possibility for manipulative conduct was remote. For good measure, it called the SEC's rejection of Grayscale's application "arbitrary and capricious."

Victory!

Now the race was on to control the next wave of the Bitcoin saga. The ruling set off a rush of other ETF issuers to win ETF approval. BlackRock, Fidelity, ARK Investments, Bitwise, and others submitted new applications for a Bitcoin ETF. Bitcoin prices surged in anticipation of the approval and the subsequent capital that was sure to follow.

In the wee small hours of January 10, Sonnenshein was at his home just outside New York. His phone started to furiously vibrate. Text after text of wire reports said the SEC had approved Grayscale's application for a Bitcoin ETF. He called his team back at the office. They were constantly refreshing the SEC's website, looking for the notice to post.

"There it is!" one of the team members screamed. Bursts of cries and clapping broke out on the phone.

"We made it!" he hollered back, stamping his feet and pumping his cell phone in the air.

On January 10, 2024, the SEC approved spot Bitcoin ETF for everyday investors. It would begin trading the next day. The team instantly shifted into action mode, activating their website properties, social and media plans, investor and internal communications; all the properties that go into launching a new product; all of which had been built in anticipation that the approval was coming.

That morning, on January 11, Sonnenshein arrived at the New York Stock Exchange following an appearance on CNBC's *Squawk Box*.

"It was like an out-of-body experience," Sonnenshein would tell colleagues. Here he was, inside one of the world's most enduring bastions of capitalism, the birthplace of the modern market, where companies like Ford and General Electric had raised the money to build America. And hanging from the rafters was the Grayscale logo he knew so well. He thought back to those client meetings that were "suddenly canceled," the condescending faces he encountered a decade ago when he'd mention to people he worked at a crypto asset management firm, the hostile interviews from journalists who simply wouldn't or couldn't accept that Bitcoin was real.

Now, because of his company's efforts, the spot Bitcoin ETF was about to go live, and his investment vehicle would list beside some of the world's best-known companies on the world's most famous exchange.

Years earlier he had toured the floor when he and his team were looking at potential listing venues, deciding if they would try to list at the New York Stock Exchange (NYSE) or the Nasdaq or Chicago Board of Options. They were all great exchanges, but nothing beats the NYSE. The sounds, the howls, the constant bustle – it's the soundtrack to money.

A smile broke out as he surveyed the grand NYSE floor. There were now only a handful of token traders who lined the floor, in stark contrast to the old busting days when traders would jockey for position or take down orders with the wink of an eye. If they were here today, they'd be screaming out orders for an ETF that tracks a product that does not exist in physical form. Progress.

And while the floor traders were largely gone, another stampede was coming.

The first day of trading was bedlam. US-listed Bitcoin ETFs saw $4.6 billion worth of shares change hands, as investors of all stripes tripped over themselves to get a piece of the action. Eleven different spot Bitcoin ETFs, including from BlackRock, Fidelity, Bitwise, and ARK, all made their debut.

BlackRock was the key. With almost $11 trillion under management, it is the world's largest asset manager. They are also the world leader in ETFs. They manage money for every investment entity in the world, including governments, pension funds, and endowments. If there is a large pool of capital looking to be deployed in the market, BlackRock is there. They offer almost every kind of investment fund known to man.

And behind it all is the founder and CEO, one Lawrence D. Fink. Fink began his career at what was then First Boston as one of the country's first bond traders. He quickly rose through the ranks to run the whole bond department. While maybe not the household name that Warren Buffett or Jamie Dimon is, the man is revered by both Wall Street and Washington and has earned a spot on the Mount Rushmore of Corporate America. When he speaks, everyone listens, from Wall and Broad to Pennsylvania Avenue. Prime ministers and presidents around the world regularly seek his advice. Market participants hang on his every word. When the financial markets nearly collapsed in 2008, the government reached out to BlackRock to help manage the crisis. In 2020, when COVID roiled the US bond market, the government again tapped Fink's BlackRock to help stabilize fixed-income markets. And his reputation on Wall Street is perhaps exceeded by his overwhelming generosity and philanthropic efforts.

He's the Godfather, plain and simple.

So when he speaks on live television, trading desks get a little quieter. People put down their phones and turn up their televisions.

And on January 12, 2023, at 6 a.m. on *Squawk Box*, Fink had a lot to say.

"I'm a believer in it," Fink told Andrew Ross Sorkin, the "it" of course being Bitcoin. It was the day after the spot Bitcoin ETF dust had settled, and Fink was sitting down to discuss earnings, a recent deal, and, of course, the smashing debut of his new ETF.

"I do believe it's an alternative source for wealth holding," he added. "I do believe it's an asset class. It's no different than what gold represented for thousands of years. It's an asset class that protects you."

Boom, there it was. Straight from the King! The CEO of the world's largest asset manager, who practically invented the modern mortgage market, who revolutionized the asset management business, who could see around corners others knew not even to look – this very same man just went on national television and said not only was he a believer in Bitcoin but that it was a viable alternative to gold, a material that had been coveted for thousands of years.

There are times in our modern age when you are bombarded with a cacophony of headlines and information. It all begins to fade into the background as one nugget of news pushes the other aside. But this could not be overstated in terms of its importance, not only because of BlackRock's role in bringing spot Bitcoin ETFs to market but also because of Fink's long and illustrious career.

Fink had made the same journey so many other investing titans had made. Just six years earlier, speaking at the Institute of International Finance, Fink said, "Bitcoin just shows you how much demand for money laundering there is in the world; that's all it is."

In the span of six years, Fink went from describing Bitcoin as "an index for money laundering" to "digital gold." Of course, Fink didn't get there overnight. It was a gradual process that was helped in part by one Robert Mitchnick, or Robbie as most people call him. Mitchnick first fell in love with crypto during a summer internship at Ripple, a digital payment company, while he was still getting his MBA from Stanford. As he often tells colleagues, it was a fortuitous stint that introduced him to the digital asset space and sparked an obsession. But as much as he believed in the power of Bitcoin to upend the traditional financial system, Mitchnick never thought it would replace it. Instead, Bitcoin was likely to exist within the system, so Mitchnick focused his work on how traditional financial services could incorporate the technology that underpinned Bitcoin, mainly the blockchain.

Soon after, BlackRock hired him for the newly created position "Head of Digital Assets" in August 2018. When he arrived, he was a stranger in a strange land. There were no other full-time employees devoted to the space. Initially, the job consisted of educating his colleagues about the potential of blockchain technology and how the firm could use it to enhance its operational capabilities. There was hardly any discussion around investing directly in Bitcoin or other coins. But in 2020 that changed, and when the firm's chief information officer (CIO) Rick Rieder began to make significant purchases in some of his portfolios, it was clear that the world's largest asset manager was ready to lean into the future.

In Fink, Mitchnick and Rieder found an open mind, which wasn't all that surprising. Unlike others, Fink's willing to change course when facts change. He is, after all, a technologist who's intellectually curious by nature. And, of course, he's a trader with a tremendous instinct for value. He would never allow previous statements to box in his firm or his clients. And now, four years later, on live television, he was making the biggest statement yet in support of Bitcoin.

Jaws dropped across the crypto universe and beyond. And then they went to work and bought as much spot Bitcoin ETFs as they could.

Most of the investor interest centered around BlackRock's and Fidelity's offerings. Within four days, BlackRock's spot Bitcoin ETF had more than $1 billion in inflows. Less than two months later, it had $10 billion in assets under management, a staggering sum to raise in such a short period. For context, State Street's industry-leading gold ETF, the GLD, has existed for nearly 20 years and has $60 billion under management.

Bitcoin, which ramped from $27 000 at the start of October to $46 000 on January 9, exploded. And it was really just a matter of supply and demand. The inflows to Bitcoin ETFs dwarfed the amount of Bitcoin being mined from the network. According to noted crypto watcher Anthony Pompliano, or Pomp as he is affectionately called, ETF inflows totaled 10 times the amount of what was mined one day following the launch.

"The price will continue going up until people stop buying it," tweeted Pomp.

One could liken Fink's appearance to those of Paul Tudor Jones and Stanley Druckenmiller two years earlier. When Druck and Tudor Jones appeared on CNBC and revealed they were buying Bitcoin, it removed any career risk for a portfolio manager to do the same. Heck, if it's good enough for those two guys, it should be good enough for us, the thinking went. And so many hedge funds and asset allocators began adding Bitcoin to their portfolios without fear of being labeled crazy. Fink's appearance and subsequent words of support for Bitcoin provided the same shelter to wealth managers and registered investment advisors, a much greater pool of capital. Had it been some crypto-native ETF issuer, then there may have been some hesitancy on the part of wealth managers to invest. But the BlackRock brand is sacrosanct, and because of that, its ETF removed the career risk of adding crypto to a client's portfolio. That's a huge amount of potential capital chasing a very limited supply of Bitcoin. It created a new permission structure.

The long-term impact of the introduction of Bitcoin ETFs is hard to quantify, but there is some precedent. When the first spot gold ETF was introduced to the market, billions of dollars that might otherwise never have been committed to gold came flooding into the space. The influx predictably drove up the price of gold, but it did something else: it damped gold's volatility. That's because unlike hedge funds, which often try to time the market and are in and out of investments, wealth managers take a longer-term approach to investing. They invest regularly and persistently and often don't try to time the market. That means that, in the aggregate, they provide a constant bid to the market. If you're wondering why stocks do nothing but go up, just look at how many more people are investing in fewer and fewer stocks. It's the same dynamic with Bitcoin.

These spot Bitcoin ETFs have only just been introduced to the market. Soon, every major wire house and large wealth manager will offer these products to their customers, unleashing an even bigger torrent of new money into this space.

It will be interesting to see if the massive drawdowns in the Bitcoin market might start to fade as more liquidity and more market participants enter the space. I suspect the price will start to grind higher in much the same fashion stocks have over the years, as more wallets come online and more money flows in.

I thought back to Brett Messing's Pacific paddle boarding conversation with Peter Briger, one of the Bitcoin OGs.

"It's really simple," Briger had said. "This thing is going to continue to be adopted, the supply is limited, and eventually more institutions will want it. And the price will go higher."

Sometimes we make investing – and life, for that matter – much harder than it needs to be. Sometimes the answer is staring you right in the face.

Looking back now, I wonder why it took me and people way smarter than I so long to fully appreciate the beauty of Bitcoin. I suspect it has to do with the bottom-up nature of its ascent. Most technologies start with the top and filter down to the masses. The US Department of Defense invented a communications network in the 1960s, and 30 years later we have the Internet, Amazon, Apple, and the rest. It started with the military, filtered on through to corporations, and before you know it, more than a billion people have an iPhone.

But with Bitcoin, it was the opposite. It started with the people dissatisfied with their government, filtered up through the financial system, was approved by the government, and now we have 11 spot Bitcoin ETFs. And that unusual progression may have fooled many professionals into not taking the asset class seriously enough.

There's a strange irony to Bitcoin's journey through the financial system. It was started by computer scientists, libertarians, and anarchists to create a form of money that existed outside the established financial construct. But to achieve its full potential, to truly become a global form of digital value, it needed to be inserted and integrated into the financial services industry. Bitcoin may have started as a brilliant idea to create a peer-to-peer payment network, but it evolved into something much bigger. It needed to in order to grow. The early days of Bitcoin consisted of people taking their coins and uploading it to their wallets. That's a wonderful concept and a remarkably useful service, but there aren't hundreds of millions of people who are technically proficient enough to grow and sustain the network in that rudimentary form. Bitcoin had to become more accessible to people who were less technically proficient. Even those same brilliant computer scientists who first played around with Bitcoin likely lost untold fortunes in lost or misplaced wallets. It needed to become easier to buy, and the only way for that to happen was for Wall Street to get involved.

In short, the only way for Bitcoin to truly achieve Satoshi's dream of being outside the financial system was for it to be able to exist as part of it. The integration of Bitcoin within the regulatory framework of Wall Street has been a good thing, maybe the best thing that could've happened to Bitcoin since it was invented. I suspect that Satoshi likely knew this, and that might explain why he made the mining process so slow and deliberate. Stretching the Bitcoin creation process over such a long period allowed the asset class to evolve over time, just as money has evolved.

This is a crucial point, and maybe something the critics miss. Bitcoin may have started as a crude peer-to-peer payment system, but like any great technology, it had the ability to grow, expand, and, most important, evolve. The Internet started as a way to send simple messages and is now the backbone of the world's economy. Think about that for a second. A technology that hardly existed 25 years ago is now at the center of pretty much every activity that we do, and the companies that were built on the Internet's promise have similarly evolved. Amazon started as a book vendor; now it sells everything. Google started to search the vast confines of the interweb. Now it's the world's biggest ad company.

In the end, the real prize was not to redefine the multi-trillion financial system but rather to help evolve it – and in so doing, provide a fantastically useful new store of value.

And just as money evolved over time, from simple shells to what exists today, I suspect Bitcoin's journey is just beginning. What it will become is anyone's guess, but for the reasons laid out in this book, I know it will be central to the world financial system in much the same way electricity and the Internet are central to the world's economies today.

If Bitcoin has taught me anything, it is to trust progress. Trust technology. Fads come and go, but progress has marked the evolution of humankind.

We are in the very early stages of this transformational story.

Chapter Sixteen

Getting Started

To paraphrase Red from *The Shawshank Redemption*, if you've read this far, maybe you're willing to read a bit further.

You now know about my journey and those of some of the smartest minds on Wall Street. Perhaps it's time to start one of your own.

So how should investors begin to think about Bitcoin as part of a personal portfolio?

Every investor is different, and of course, you should always consult a financial advisor before making any investment. Having said that, I believe Bitcoin should have an essential role in *everyone's* portfolio. You should view crypto as you would any asset class, just like stocks, bonds, real estate, or gold. A portfolio without Bitcoin is not a balanced portfolio. Now, that's not to say Bitcoin should occupy the same percentage as stocks or bonds, but it should be a core holding, and as with any asset, its allocation should be adjusted quarterly or at least annually.

I think 2–5% of your overall portfolio is a good place to start. If things go south, it won't hurt you too much. But if it takes off, it can dramatically change your life. Imagine if you had a $100 000 portfolio and you allocated $2000 to Bitcoin in 2014. That $2000 alone would be worth about $350 000 today, assuming you held the whole way. Even if the other 98% of your portfolio had stayed flat over that time, you'd have made a fortune.

Now of course, any disciplined investor would likely have sold some of that Bitcoin along the way, if only to keep its allocation in your portfolio in line with your original targets, which is prudent. But it's a risk well worth taking in my opinion, and the risk profile is one not too different from owning stocks.

I can already feel the hate, so let me explain.

Meta, the parent company of Facebook, a core holding in pretty much any balanced portfolio, went from $388 in the fall of 2021 to $85 in October 2023. It's now at $532, and the company is worth north of a trillion dollars. Meta is one of the world's most widely held stocks and covered by

45 analysts on Wall Street, most of whom have it at a strong buy with an average price target north of $500. How can that same stock, which in theory should be well understood by the investment community, lose 80% of its value in a year and then gain 200%? This isn't some tiny biotech stock. This is Meta, owner of Facebook, Instagram, and WhatsApp!

It's simple and a lesson I learned many years ago: most guys on Wall Street, particularly those with the fanciest clothes from the fanciest firms, are often wrong.

It's true! That's not to say they're not smart or not worth listening to. They are. But don't take anything they say as gospel, and like anything in life, if the consensus is too far to one side, you're probably better moving to the other.

Bitcoin is volatile. So is Meta. So is Amazon, which experienced multiple declines of 70% or more before becoming a dominant trillion-dollar company. Nvidia went from $30 to $10 to $140 in the span of two years. Should you not own it? You might say, "Stocks are too volatile. I can't own them in my portfolio. I need something real, like commodities or housing."

Fair enough. But if you're in that camp, I would gently point you to April 20, 2020. At around 12:30 p.m. Eastern standard time that day, as stocks were tumbling amid a torrent of COVID-related horrible economic news, something unthinkable happened. The price of a barrel of West Texas Intermediate (WTI) fell $55.90 to settle at a negative $37.62

a barrel. Many traders had to do a double take: how can a barrel of oil go negative?

The answer is complicated and has to do with the technicalities of futures trading, but the broader point here is that any asset can crash and rise again. Volatility should not be a reason to avoid an asset class. Reserve currencies move slowly day to day, but over time, they can lose half their value. Just look at the Japanese yen over the past decade.

The point is simple: any asset can crash, so volatility isn't really a good reason to avoid it. Instead, ask yourself if it will be part of the future. Will it solve the problems of tomorrow? And perhaps most important, can you afford not to own it? Had you not owned Apple shares between 2010 and 2020, you were effectively short the market. Best to ask instead how much of something you should own. And no matter your risk tolerance, 2% of a portfolio makes sense to me.

Start Small: No Rush

Like any position, there is no need to buy everything all at once. If you came into $100000, you wouldn't go out and spend it all on stocks. You'd scale into it, and I think the same approach works for establishing a position in Bitcoin. Scale into the position on a regular basis. Maybe every quarter you commit a certain amount to Bitcoin and dollar-cost your way into your target position.

Now, sticking with the previous example, if you have a $100000 portfolio, it's not unreasonable to have 2% of it, or $2000, in Bitcoin if you consider yourself a conservative investor. The best way to establish that position is to buy Bitcoin in quarterly increments of $500 until you've reached your target allocation, which in this case would be $2000. This will protect and allow you to use Bitcoin's inherent volatility to your advantage. In a given year, Bitcoin can have multiple drawdowns of 20% or more. But if you're regularly committing capital to establishing your position, your weighted cost will likely be considerably lower than it would have been had you established the entire position at once. So, don't fear Bitcoin's volatility. Instead, harness it and make it work for you by taking advantage of sharp selloffs.

But if you're not a conservative investor and you lean a bit toward growth in your portfolio, you should consider increasing that allocation to something closer to 10%. That might seem high, but if you're a growth investor, having a simple 2% exposure won't provide the real benefits of owning a growth asset. Imagine identifying Apple as a can't-miss investment and committing only 2% of your money to it. Trust me when I say all the money in the world will not assuage the regret of not buying more. If you're utterly wrong, 10% won't kill you. If Bitcoin stays flat, that 10% allocation won't kill you either. But if it goes significantly higher, which I think it will, that 10% will change your life.

Now, there are some investors who describe themselves as *Bitcoin maximalists*. They can't own enough. To them, 55% of their portfolio is in Bitcoin. Saylor puts himself in that camp. To be a Bitcoin maximalist is to believe it is less risky to own Bitcoin than to not. These investors believe Bitcoin already is a diversified bet on the future, so there is no need to own anything else. By their logic, it's silly to own a slice of the future and commit anything less than 50% of their available capital. Only you can determine which camp you're in, but if you're completely new to this asset class and a conservative investor, start small and gradually increase your exposure as your comfort level grows.

Target Reached – Now What?

OK, you've established your asset allocation position through diligent and disciplined purchases. And now something great happens. Bitcoin surges. To the moon, as they say. When you open your statement, you see something great. Bitcoin is now a much bigger percentage of your portfolio because it's appreciated so much. What do you do? This is what you call a high-class problem, and it is my sincerest hope you experience it multiple times in your life.

This is more a personal decision and one for which you should consult with a financial advisor. But for me, it comes down to how much of a believer you are in Bitcoin. If you believe, as I do, that Bitcoin will hit $500000, don't sell. If you need to, sell your initial $2000 so you're now playing with house money. That's how you achieve generational wealth. If you bought $200 worth of Apple in 2001 and held it until today, you'd be sitting on more than $700000. That's life-changing. Had you bought $10000 worth and held it, you'd be reading this book from a beach somewhere really nice and expensive. The point being, if you're a true believer, sell only to pay for weddings and bar mitzvahs. Keep the rest. I suspect it could change your life.

Now, if you are not a true believer and you're one of these people who will obsessively check your account every five minutes, perhaps it might be best for you to stick to your allocation plan. In this case, check your portfolio at set times a year, either quarterly or semi-annually and make sure your Bitcoin is not becoming too large a position. If it is, sell to right-size that position to your target allocation. This way you'll be selling into strength, not weakness.

If Bitcoin falls – and trust me, it will and it will seem painful – use that sell-off as an opportunity to add Bitcoin until it hits your target. Much like dollar-cost averaging, this will allow you to buy weakness and add to your positions at opportune times. Sell into strength and buy into weakness to make sure your Bitcoin holdings are in line with your asset allocation strategy. For what it's worth, you should be doing this with all the assets in your portfolio. If your model calls for you to be 60/40 stocks to bonds and the equity portion of your portfolio has grown to 80%, look to trim some of those gains and deploy those proceeds according to your asset allocation plan.

Only you can make this decision, but trust that Bitcoin will be a core holding, and know that by selling, you could be making the same move many investors did with Apple and Nvidia before those companies made their generational marches higher. If Bitcoin has taught me anything, it is to trust progress. Trust technology. Fads come and go, but progress has marked the evolution of humankind.

And it's going up!

Exchange-Traded Funds, Futures, or Bitcoin?

It's probably never been easier to start investing in Bitcoin. We've detailed how the pioneers in this space have made buying or selling Bitcoin a process that is now almost indistinguishable from that of buying and selling stocks. You select a broker that offers Bitcoin and Bitcoin-related products, download the software to either your phone or your computer, wire the money from your bank account, and you'll be up and running in five minutes. And there are a number of terrific broker dealers that offer crypto services including Fidelity, Coinbase, Robin Hood, TastyTrade, and

Interactive Brokers, among others. Some are better suited for active traders, but to me, trading is needlessly hard and a very expensive hobby. Timing any market, let alone one as volatile as Bitcoin, is a fool's errand. Best to stick to your asset allocation plan and rebalancing.

Once you're up and running, you're going to be faced with your first real choice: do you buy Bitcoin directly, Bitcoin Futures, or Bitcoin exchange-traded funds (ETFs)?

I think your level of technical and financial expertise should dictate how you choose exposure to this asset class. Futures are primarily for institutional and self-directed retail investors who are firmly in the advanced swim camp. Market makers and liquidity providers will often look to the futures market to hedge existing positions. If you regularly trade futures, like the E-mini S&P 500 Index Futures, Bitcoin futures might be a way for you to get exposure to the asset class, and the product offers a capital-efficient way to make a leveraged bet on the direction of Bitcoin, from either the short or long side. But trading futures can be complicated; you have expiration dates that require you to roll your contract out, at least in the United States. And at the end of the day, they are a derivative of Bitcoin, so while it closely tracks the prices of spot Bitcoin, there are times where market forces can push it out of whack. But if you are a sophisticated investor, the low margin requirements make Bitcoin futures an efficient way to express a leveraged view on the underlying asset.

That brings us to ETFs. This is fast emerging as a hot topic for many crypto enthusiasts. Again, I think this decision depends on your comfort and level of investment sophistication. Some in the OG camp think Bitcoin is a better alternative to spot Bitcoin ETFs because with Bitcoin, you actually own the coin. If you want to transfer it or take control through a self-custody wallet, like a Fidelity or Coinbase, then you can do that and take your Bitcoin off-chain (more on that in a second). With Bitcoin ETFs, you don't actually own the Bitcoin, in much the same way that if you owned the gold ETF GLD, you wouldn't actually own gold bars. What you can do is sell those ETFs (Bitcoin or anything else) for US dollars. For most people who are more accustomed to reading standard monthly statements, spot Bitcoin ETFs might be more familiar and comfortable. ETFs also provide a level of efficiency, particularly for crypto novices. You buy them just as you would a stock, and sell them the same way, with the cash sitting there in your account. The bid-ask spreads for ETFs are tight. There's great liquidity, and you will be well served by expressing your Bitcoin investment views through ETFs. They're inexpensive, secure, and easy. For most investors, this will be the easiest on-ramp to the digital world.

And now to the real thing. I'm a purist and a professional money manager with decades of experience. I prefer to own Bitcoin outright. With all the crypto advancements in the financial services spaces, owning Bitcoin through Fidelity Digital Assets or Coinbase or Robinhood is straightforward enough that most people will have no problems. Owning Bitcoin outright will avail you of many of its embedded advantages that we've discussed so far. You can transfer money cheaply to any party around the world. You can transport large sums of value easily.

But I would suggest maybe even taking it a step further. If you really want to understand crypto, you might find it instructive to take the journey as the journey was originally intended. In other words, experience it the way someone might have 10 or 15 years ago. I would liken this process to learning to drive a manual transmission. It's a bit more onerous, but it's fun, and you'll learn more about driving. Again, I would not recommend this unless you're technically proficient, and I'd only use a small amount of money at first until you feel more comfortable with the technology.

But try transferring money to a wallet. This wallet will have two keys, a public and a private one. The public key is the address to receive and send Bitcoin. The private key is used to access that Bitcoin. You can store these keys to a connected device, which is called *hot storage*, or store them on an unconnected device, which is called *cold storage* and considered safer. The danger, of course, is that you might forget your password to the wallet. This process is akin to removing cash from your bank account and storing it in a safe in your house. Again, there's not a tremendous amount of practicality to doing it, but it is an interesting and educational experience.

Most brokerages that offer crypto services give you the ability to transfer your Bitcoin to a wallet, and creating a wallet address is as easy as creating an email. But from an investment standpoint, you're fine simply buying Bitcoin in any of the previously mentioned brokerage accounts and just letting it be, tending to it quarterly or annually to make sure it's in line with your asset allocation plan.

Up, Down, Sideways

You've opened your account, you've wired in your fiat money, and now you're ready to make a trade. The question now is what makes Bitcoin go in one direction or another? There really is no right answer to this question other than to say whether there are buyers or sellers. After all, there is no intrinsic value to Bitcoin. But over time, investors have identified a number of factors that have pushed Bitcoin one way or the other.

In general, Bitcoin is widely considered to be insurance against fiat debasement and periods of hyperinflation. It's also a speculative asset and as such tends to trade alongside high-growth tech stocks like Nvidia. So periods of risk-off, where global demand for dollars is high, tend to depress Bitcoin prices, just as it does for other commodities, like gold and oil. Use these opportunities to add to Bitcoin, particularly if its asset allocation is below your target. Extreme bond market volatility, which also correlates to risk-off periods in the market, also tends to weigh on Bitcoin as well.

This is all a fancy way of saying that Bitcoin is driven by liquidity itself. Bitcoin should perform well when there is a lot of global liquidity and risk assets are performing well. The Fed's easing cycles are periods where Bitcoin might deserve another look. Bitcoin should benefit when the Fed expands its balance sheet in the hopes of getting the economy going. The more liquidity, the more risk, and, ideally, the more gains for your Bitcoin.

Of course, these conditions might influence Bitcoin in the short-term, but in the long term, as we've discussed, Bitcoin will continue to benefit as more and more investors deem it a necessary alternative to traditional fiat currencies. But in terms of short-term inflection points, when you're looking for entry points or just trying to understand why Bitcoin is moving, there are some basic techniques, and although methodologies often evolve over time, a couple are still worth considering.

The Cost of Producing Bitcoin

As we explained earlier in the book, the Bitcoin miners who verify transactions and maintain the network are rewarded for their work by winning the block and receiving Bitcoin.

But there is a considerable cost to that activity, mainly the electricity necessary to power the computers that are verifying all the transactions. Remember, they are solving for millions of complicated equations. In fact, according to the University of Cambridge Electricity Consumption Index, Bitcoin mining used 121 terawatt-hours of electricity in 2023. That's about the same amount that the entire country of the Netherlands (population 17 million) used in 2022. The point is this stuff adds up, and one good measure to tell if Bitcoin is fairly valued on a short-term basis is to look at the cost of production versus the price of a coin. You can think of it as the break-even point for miners. While not always connected, mining costs can sometimes be a tell on the Bitcoin price. In general, higher mining costs are supportive of Bitcoin prices because it becomes unprofitable to mine and there are fewer coins being extracted, lessening the overall supply. Remember, there are only 21 million Bitcoins available to be mined, and just shy of 20 million have been mined. When mining costs fall, it becomes cheaper to mine Bitcoin, and that could lead to an increase in supply. As a rule of thumb, when the price of Bitcoin is two times the cost of production, that's a sign that Bitcoin may have run too far in the short term. Admittedly, this methodology was more useful when the space was new and there were fewer coins, but it's useful to look at and observe.

Costs Basis/Charts

Another metric that some find useful is the weighted average cost of Bitcoin held in wallets. Some investors like to think of that as the long-term cost basis of owning Bitcoin. In some ways, it acts as a floor. If Bitcoin is above an investor's cost basis, that person might feel less incentive to sell. If it's below, investors might want to cut their losses.

Technical analysis also can be a good metric for short-term price inflections. Many Bitcoin investors do look to traditional chart formations to glean near-term price action. Head and shoulders tops, wedges, and other classic patterns can all be good tells for near-term moves.

But, again, the best strategy is not to trade it but rather own it and continue to add when it falls below your target allocation level.

Chapter Seventeen

Your Journey

Is BITCOIN GOLD OR a payment system? I think that's sort of a false choice. There have been multiple bullish narratives that have propelled shares of Apple, Nvidia, and Amazon higher through the years. Once upon a time, the bull thesis for Nvidia was tied to graphic chips. Now it's artificial intelligence (AI). Amazon used to sell books. Now it sells storage for the cloud, video, and anything else you can imagine, because at the end of the day, it is simply a vessel for innovation and disruption. And if history has shown anything, it's that those two ingredients can be tremendously lucrative.

At the end of the day, I'm just glad to be able to play a small part in this gigantic technological and financial story. Sure, I've made a few shekels by investing in Bitcoin, but that's really not the point. Don't roll your eyes – it's true! What I treasure most is being able to open other people's eyes.

I still remember when, in the heat of the Bitcoin mania, the manager of a Middle East sovereign wealth fund called me up to offer his congratulations. I told him that while we'd put a lot of thought into our long-term thesis, our quick gains could sort of be chalked up to some lucky timing. But he was insistent. "You've helped pull us into the future," he said, "and we're thrilled to be part of it with you."

The future is fast spreading in the asset management business. In May 2024, the State of Wisconsin revealed through a filing that the Wisconsin State Pension Fund purchased nearly $160 million worth of Bitcoin via the BlackRock and Grayscale spot Bitcoin exchange-traded funds (ETFs). What was most remarkable was the timing of the purchase, almost immediately after the ETFs were introduced. While giving no reason for the purchase, earlier press reports noted that in recent years the fund's manager, Edwin Denson, had increased the fund's exposure to inflation-sensitive assets. The fund has $150 billion under management. Although the Wisconsin State Pension Fund was the first, it likely won't be the last. As discussed earlier, the introduction of ETFs has made it easier for nontraditional Bitcoin buyers to participate in the crypto markets, and as the asset class becomes more mainstream, it will increasingly play a role in sovereign and pension funds looking for a hedge against central bank currency debasement. In late 2021, El Salvador became the first country to accept Bitcoin as legal tender. The country's president, Nayib Bukele, said the move would spur investment and economic growth through extending "traditional financial services" to nearly 70% of Salvadorians who are unbanked. Bukele has credited the adoption with a surge in tourism as well as with a surge in Salvadorians sending money back into the country, or remittances. It is likely that other countries with unstable financial systems will look to Bitcoin to impart stability to their respective financial systems.

And as more entities adopt Bitcoin, more creative uses for it will emerge. Will it become the first global currency? Will it be used to colonize the moon or Mars? It's not inconceivable that a truly digital currency will have more utility on foreign planets. Who knows. We do know that it has accomplished in 15 years what it's taken centuries for other currencies or stores of value to achieve. We do know that it continues to be adopted and embraced along the economic scale. And I think it's safe to say we do know it will continue to be embraced by Wall Street.

Your children may be more comfortable in a tokenized financial economy – buying sports tickets, houses, and collectables using the blockchain and digital assets – in much the same way they are more comfortable navigating an iPhone than they are a television set. Their world is virtual, a series of ones and zeros.

When my son AJ calls now, I can discuss the intricacies of the blockchain with him. I now understand the Internet of Things. I'm proud to say that I took the journey and opened my mind to a completely new way of looking at finance and value. I'm prouder, still, to admit that there is still much I don't know. I am open and excited to see how this space will evolve and to see which of my current beliefs will be challenged.

I hope you are, too. After all, anything that goes from $0.01 to $70 000 probably has better days ahead.

Acknowledgments

~

THE VALUE OF A network is directly proportional to the number of parties engaged. Robert Metcalfe taught us that. Bitcoin taught us that, too. And my life is proof of that. Much like Bitcoin, my journey would not have been possible without an amazing network that supported me each step of the way.

Giles Anderson, my fabulous book agent, encouraged me to find and share my voice from the beginning. I would also like to thank my friends at Wiley who came to me with this project. You showed great faith in me, and I hope I delivered.

A ton of thanks to the incredible people within the crypto community who guided me through me the world of the Coin, including but not limited to Peter Diamandis,

Mike Novogratz, Wences Casares, Michael Sonnenshein, Pete Briger, Michael Saylor, and Terry Duffy. Every day I am inspired by the great work of my longtime friend and partner Brett Messing and, of course, the great team behind us at SkyBridge. You are all ambassadors to progress, and I'm proud to call you my colleagues. I'm prouder, still, to call you my friends. A special shout out to my friends at CNBC, KC Sullivan, Dan Colarusso, Mary Duffy, Scott Wapner, the great crew Squawk Box, including Andrew Ross Sorkin, Becky Quick, Joe Kernen, Anne Tironi and Jacqueline Corba. I'd also like to acknowledge my longtime friend and writing partner, Maxwell Meyers. He gets my voice.

Most important, I would be nowhere without the Scaramucci network, which is vast, colorful, and a source of much joy. Thank you to my beautiful wife Deirdre. You make my life possible and fill it with truth and goodness. You make the world a better place. Never stop being you. To my older kids, AJ, Anthony, and Amelia, I love you. I could not be prouder of the way you have each lived your lives. To the latest vintage, James and Nick, you inspire and remind me that life is always about new adventures and new beginnings. To my parents, Alexander and Marie, everything I am is because of you. And what more could I say than that?

About the Author

~

Anthony Scaramucci is the founder and managing partner of SkyBridge, a global alternative investment firm. He is also the founder and chairman of SALT, a global thought leadership forum and venture studio. He started his career on Wall Street at Goldman Sachs in the late 1980s and was appointed Vice President of Wealth Management in 1993. After Goldman, Scaramucci founded Oscar Capital Management, which was later acquired by Neuberger Berman. In addition to his many appearances on CNBC, CNN, MSNBC, and Fox, Scaramucci also hosts the podcast *Open Book with Anthony Scaramucci* and is the author of several books. He briefly served as White House Communications Director. He is a Tuft University and Harvard Law School graduate and lives in Manhasset, Long Island, with his family.